What Fellow Trainers and Leading Entrepreneurs Say About Scott Schilling and His 'Heart-Centered' Selling Methods for Business Audiences...

"Scott Schilling's Heart-Centered Approach to Selling is exactly what this country and the world needs right now. Coming from the Heart with the intention to serve, rather than to simply get, is not only more fulfilling; it is more effective. Being a go-giver rather than a go-getter is the new paradigm for where we are. People want to be sincerely served, not sold. They want to be truly cared for, not taken advantage of.

Scott is a master at this because this is where he lives from. His ability to teach his Heart-Centered approach to selling and to life is inspiring. Scott has presented his Heart-Centered approach to enrollment and sales at several of my seminars, and the participants were thrilled and enthusiastic about what they learned. I highly recommend his books, audio-programs and seminars."

Jack Canfield
Co-creator of the *Chicken Soup for the Soul* series, co-author of *The Success Principles: How to Get from Where You Are to Where You Want to Be*, and featured teacher in the movie, *The Secret.*

"Scott Schilling reaches you in a unique and inspiring manner. As we all think we have solid, experienced-based approaches to selling and marketing products and/or services, Scott works closely with you to methodically examine your current approaches, strategies and techniques and helps you construct more effective methods.

Because he identifies with you and your practices on a personal level, his efforts lead to (1) enhancements that are easily assimilated and implemented, and (2) contributions that are clearly measurable."

Paul E. Fulchino
Chairman, President, and CEO Aviall, Inc / A Wholly-Owned Boeing Company

"Scott is a salesmen's--salesman, he is a master at selling and teaching selling. Go way out of your way to study with this master."

Mark Victor Hansen
Co-creator of the *Chicken Soup for the Soul* series

1

"Scott is the Master in the Art and Science of selling. I have seen him in action dozens of times and I am in awe of what he does and how he does it.... and even more impressive are the consistent results he gets. Even though it looks like magic, Scott knows exactly what he is doing and now he is willing to teach you the secrets he has spent years perfecting. Ignore Scott's wisdom and teaching at your peril."

Keith J. Cunningham
Entrepreneurial Expert—Author of *Keys to the Vault* www.keystothevault.com

"Scott Schilling has spent decades studying and perfecting his art, and in doing so has become a true master of relationship-building.

In his new book *Without Clients...Ya Got Nothin'* Scott provides a strong position for how the power of the human spirit, based in service, is the way to improve the world condition. Scott is one who truly embodies the principle 'Loving Service—My First Technique.' I have experienced this personally; now it's your turn."

Dr. Gilles Lamarche
Vice President, Development and External Relations - Parker University

"Scott's dynamic approach to success coaching will inspire and uplift the soul. I have experienced first-hand his entrancing insights, which have empowered me and his many audiences. Scott embodies sincerity and compassion toward others, with knowledge and skills he willingly and selflessly imparts. It's clear he loves what he does, and it shows as he helps others."

C. Neil Linton
Entrepreneur and Educator

"The best testimony for the quality of Scott's work with our sales staff at our hotels is that two years later they still speak of what they learned and use it."

Richard and Andrea Goeglein
Co-owners—Evening Star Holdings

"Scott's selling ideas are the best I have seen made available. They just simply work! For those who don't think they are 'salespeople' but have to 'sell' every day to grow their practices, these ideas will give you the comfort you need. Presenting what you have to offer favorably and 'selling' has never been this easy."

Dr. Fabrizio Mancini
President—Parker University, Author of the best-seller *The Power of Self-Healing*

"Scott is passionate, focused and driven and follows through with 100% commitment on whatever he sets his mind to do. It is awesome to see someone out in the field creating transformation in so many lives who has started by transforming his own."

JJ Virgin
Celebrity Health and Nutrition Expert

"I've known Scott for years and watched his effectiveness with students and audiences alike. He exquisitely conveys the concept of 'selling without selling' that is easy to understand and implement. He will show you how to grow your business, period. I highly recommend him."

Shawne Duperon
6 Time Emmy Winner—Networking, Media and Gossip Expert

"Scott Schilling is not only one of my Best Friends; he's also one of THE best professional speakers I've ever heard on any stage. If he ever offers you his expertise on selling without making people feel uncomfortable, grab it like a lifeline."

Rhea Perry
Founder of Entrepreneur Days and www.EducatingforSuccess.com

"Scott Schilling is an extraordinary business mentor and trainer! His authentic, real approach is so easy to grasp you'll be selling more in a Heartbeat."

Teresa de Grosbois
President of Wildfire Workshops & Founder of the Evolutionary Business Council

"I've known Scott for years and seen audiences respond to his presentations and run to take advantage of what he was offering. He not only teaches providing quality solutions to those you present to, but uses the very strategies and techniques he teaches himself to serve his audiences."

Rick Frishman
Publisher—Morgan James Publishing

"Scott Schilling has rocked the house multiple times on my stages. He comes from the Heart, presents with passion and demonstrates the very sales skills he teaches. His 'Without Clients…Ya Got Nothin' details how anyone can achieve the sales results they desire by putting these quick, easy and effective lessons into action."

T. Harv Eker
#1 N.Y. Times Bestselling Author of *Secrets of the Millionaire Mind*

"Scott Schilling's consistent results prove his capability as a salesperson, but what I admire most about Scott is HOW he sells. He has taught me that effective selling comes from the Heart, is always focused on the needs of the customer and never needs to be pushy. Scott has a sales mind-set and the ability to teach others how to develop theirs; I'm proud to call him my teacher and my friend."

Robert MacPhee
Author of *Manifesting for Non-Gurus*

"I have had the pleasure of sitting under Scott's instruction on several occasions. There are those who can 'sell' and there are those who can 'teach you to sell.' But rare is the person who can do both and do so truly from the Heart. This is Scott's true niche, in my opinion."

Jeff McKissack
Founder—Defense by Design & Author of *Power Proverbs for Personal Defense*

"I am honored to have known Scott Schilling since 2008. I was fortunate to attend several of Scott's Selling Courses and I recall making the following observations:

Scott Schilling is a consummate gentleman and he prepares himself like a professional athlete. Scott is passionate about making a measurable difference in the quality of people's lives. Scott's energy, passion and enthusiasm are infectious and his sales business wisdom is unparalleled.

Anyone at any level will learn how to raise their sales game through Scott's proven sales methodology and Ideas. Anyone seeking to become stronger sales leaders will benefit from Scott's unique expertise in the art, craft and magic of selling."

Michael Hutchison
Co-Founder, Immersive CRM—Author, *Speaking Mastery: 7 Keys to Delivering High Impact Presentations*

"Scott Schilling exemplifies excellence in sales effectiveness! He has the ability to communicate and motivate people to take action on his ideas and implement them to achieve their personal best! His approach is down to earth and represents his values and principles of being in service to others and gives of himself unselfishly!"

Bill Nardiello
Chairman-Board of Trustees-Parker University

"I met Scott after interviewing him on my radio show, Smart Women Talk Radio. Though he wasn't a typical guest, aka a woman! He was excellent in both the information he delivered as well as his delivery. As I listened to him, I realized I wanted to hire him as my next coach.

In the months we've been working together the greatest value he brings me is in his ability to distill the stories and issues in my business and life into lessons that linger long after the story is told. Clarity, focus, faith, and trust in the process, have all been deepened through our weekly calls.

I unconditionally recommend Scott if you're looking for a coach that will challenge you to own your deepest held beliefs, take action on your biggest dreams, and want a partner who believes that the best is yet to come.

Thank you Scott for your coaching!"

Victoria Trabosh
Executive Coach and Author of ***Dead Rita's Wisdom***

"Scott, is one of the best sales trainers and action taking sales genius on the planet. His integrity and compassion for others is underrated. Scott is someone you want to emulate and learn from. His drive, commitment to action, completion and making sure everyone wins is what every sales organizations and business needs, desires and strives for. If ever in need of "sales training on steroids" Call Scott" Scott is also a bestselling author, highly desired speaker and creator of "Talking with Giants". Scott is also a great friend, mentor and coach."

Jacob Roig
Owner and Head Coach—Luminary Coaching Services

"I have worked with Scott in a couple of different networking groups. Scott is a brilliant Speaker and Teacher. His ideas on how to grow your business and personal life are based on solid Christian Principles with perhaps the best application of these principles that I have seen. Stick with Scott...you will learn something!"

Tom Parker
Vice President—K&H Insurance Services

Create more relationships...

Provide better solutions...

Achieve greater results...

Enjoy every bit of it!

Without Clients...Ya Got Nothin'!

104 Powerful Ideas to Get More Clients

Scott Schilling
Business Growth Expert

www.ScottSchilling.com

To my amazing wife Peggy,

Thank you for your loving support of all my endeavors

allowing me to follow my dreams and passion.

To my two wonderful children Taylor and Jordan,

for being an inspiration to me in the way

you live following God's path for your lives.

To the many friends and mentors

that have been there throughout my career to

guide me, teach me and share your wisdom.

Welcome!

I have to admit, I'm extremely excited that you took the action to invest in yourself and have started digging into *"Without Clients...Ya Got Nothin'!"* This work has been far too long in coming, but like most things, the timing and opportunities created by its release now are phenomenal!

By taking control of your own knowledge regarding customer behavior and the sales process, you will immediately become better. Buckminster Fuller said, "You can't learn less!" Just by studying the material, your skill-set will increase. As you put things you learn into action, your mindset will improve. And as your success grows, you will become more fulfilled both personally and professionally.

I've been blessed to be a professional salesperson since age 18 when I became a licensed Life Insurance Agent. Actually, my first selling experience happened as a 4 year old wandering up and down the aisles of an Amtrak train going from Wisconsin to California. I was selling tickets to the people on the train...scribbling something on a piece of paper...exchanging it for a few coins. That's right...I sold them tickets to a train they were already on!

The last six years I have had the opportunity to speak nearly 1,500 times across the country and around the world. In that time, I sold over $20 million worth of products from the platform to people that for the most part, I had never met before.

To accomplish that task, you have to be able to create a relationship, sometimes from afar, and get your audience to know you, like you and trust you quickly. The reason I'm so excited right now is because the exact same process I used to accomplish those great results are included here in this book.

It takes hard work and dedication to become a successful sales professional. By reading this, you have obviously taken at least the first step on your path to greater results. For even more information, know that there are always resources available to help you improve.

Please feel free to drop by **www.ScottSchilling.com** from time to time. There is plenty of free material to help you expand your knowledge base.

Sign up for my free newsletter "Selling is Serving!" Check out the blogs; explore the thought of attending a live event, and just plain stay in touch! I have written many articles, blogs, guides, reports and other pieces of information all designed to pass along what I have learned throughout my career. I learned a long time ago that we can't take it with us...but we can share it to shape the future!

I'd like to say "Thank You" in advance for reading this material and investing in your future. If you have any questions, comments or simply need a little guidance getting from where you are to where you want to be, please don't hesitate to contact me. Your interest, enthusiasm and desire to succeed are inspiring!

To Your Increasing Success!

Scott Schilling

www.ScottSchilling.com
Scott@ScottSchilling.com

Table of Contents

*"Destiny is not a matter of chance, but of choice.
Not something to wish for, but to attain."*
William Jennings Bryan

Welcome to "Without Clients…Ya Got Nothin!"

Thank you for taking the time to invest in yourself and the many people you will help along the way by reading this book and putting what you learn into action.

If you think this book is going to teach you how to "sell," it's not! If you think you have to be a "master selling machine," you don't! At least not in the way you have thought about it or been taught to do it in the past. By picking up this book in the first place, you obviously resonate with the life concept of being of service. I'll bet you would love to do better so you can do more for others and yourself. Call it a hunch.

How do I know? Pretty simple actually, most people I have had the pleasure to meet throughout my life have a true desire to love and be loved, help and be helped, and do their part in living a fulfilling happy life through their efforts.

Whether you are a seasoned sales professional looking to refresh and rediscover your zest for your profession, or someone who doesn't see themselves as a salesperson and yet is dependent upon talking with others to create and maintain their revenue stream, this book is for you!

The reality is we are all "selling" every minute of every day. More than likely you have never thought of it that way, but it's true. You just haven't framed it that way in your head to this point. Think about it, have you ever put a child to bed? You made a sale! Have you ever been on a date? You made a sale! Are you married? You're better at selling than you thought. Look at the product with which you had to work and you finalized that one.

The true desire of this work is to demystify selling and help you gain new awareness and connect further with your "inner salesperson" as you apply this information. To help you see the growth that is available to you, let's take a look at the nine dot test below and on the next page.

Here are the instructions: With your pencil never leaving the paper once you start solving the puzzle, draw four straight lines, and connect all nine dots. Most people, after a bit of thought, can see the answer.

● ● ●

● ● ●

● ● ●

You can start at the upper left hand dot, proceed right to the lower right hand dot, turn left and go past the farthest left dot, come back up on a 45 degree angle through the second dot on the left and the second dot on the top line, and then back down through the right hand side, finishing by connecting the three dots on the right.

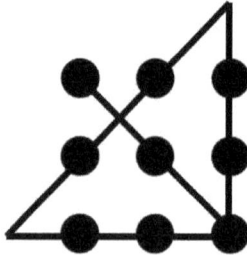

The solution really isn't that hard once you see it. The key is it causes you to think outside the box, outside the original paradigm you see based on the original design of the nine dots. A paradigm is simply a set of rules by which you make decisions. Its width and breadth are determined by your life experiences and knowledge gained to date. Your ability to "stretch" the walls of your paradigm is what enables you to grow and become an even better you.

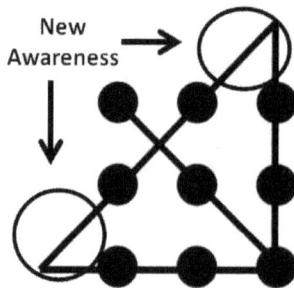

New Awareness

The areas past the original paradigm are termed "new awareness." This is where the learning takes place and the exciting part is that the area of this new awareness actually gets geometrical. It can expand to places you may never have thought possible. There is so much room to push the boundaries of your mind to greater levels it is amazing. Places of greater service, love, fulfillment and more.

Stretching you is one of the goals of "Without Clients." I want to challenge you to look at how you have done things in the past, incorporate key enhancements you learn along the way, and "sell" with greater quality, ease and satisfaction along the way.

So with that, let's explore this type of stretching. Let me ask a question, "What's the world's oldest profession?" Shame on some of you! Its sales! There was no other act before an agreement was made to finalize a transaction. That's a sale.

The definition of sales is simple. Webster's dictionary lists it as, "An exchange of products, goods or services for an amount of money or its equivalent." Bingo, we've already identified one of the issues "Heart-Centered" people face with traditional sales training. To accomplish what they need to accomplish, they have to go after the money. For many of you that's hard, because you really want to do so much good in the world. I want you to do (good) in the world as well. No, that's actually not true. I want you to do (great) in the world!

It is only through your presenting what you have to offer and having others take you up on that offer, that both the world and you will prosper. We need you, we need what you have to offer, we need your contribution to humanity, and you need to receive the value for who you are, what you offer and what it will do for all associated with it.

So let's start learning right out of the blocks. Let's use the second part of the definition of sales, the "or its equivalent" part. By definition, it is possible to focus on how it makes your Heart feel as "the equivalent." Simply reframing the context of what a sale is within your mind converts you from selling to serving. Exchanging what you have to offer to those that need it is essential to both parties. And, oh by the way, along with making your Heart feel good, your sales prospect received the product, service, enrolled in the cause or offering you represent, and you received the value you deserved for it. All by modifying your focus, cool huh?

The definition I teach of sales is simple. It is *"Education through Communication without Manipulation."* It is your task to be true educators of what you have to offer. To be truly successful in "selling" any products, services, cause or offering, you have to change your mindset of selling into a Heartset of serving the customer by providing a solution to their needs, wants and desires. It is the "Heart connection" that creates and develops life-long relationships and Clients for life.

So many times, sales management or management in general looks at ROI, the "Return on Investment" to be the determinant as to monies spent, people hired and actions taken. What I believe should be a major consideration in the decision making process is ROR, the "Return on Relationships!" Ultimately when you initiate and grow relationships within the context of growing your business, you will be more successful, be more fulfilled and significantly happier.

More importantly, it helps all involved live the two reasons I believe we have all been put on earth in the first place: first to have a fabulous life, and second to help as many other people as we can along the way. When you work to serve each other, magic happens!

What you will learn is how to create an "environment for people to buy" what you have to offer. The offering could be a physical product, retaining your services or even supporting a cause that is near and dear to your Heart. While in all cases, selling and creating an environment to buy create a transaction of some sort, the dynamics during and after your interaction are very different.

The biggest difference is the orientation of the presentation. Selling is sales person or seller oriented. However when you create an environment to buy, the presentation is customer oriented. As you will learn, to be truly successful, it's WIIFT—What's in it for Them! They make the decision to buy; they feel good about their decision; they love what you have to offer, and they love you throughout the entire process. Sounds nice doesn't it?

This book is especially written for the many people who are working to serve humanity and do good things in the world. Because of their orientation towards being "Heart-Centered," they may not have the selling or presentation skill-set necessary to achieve the results they truly desire. More importantly, many times "Heart-Centered" people do not receive the value they deserve for the quality and commitment they deliver to their mission and humanity. That's just plain B.S. - Bad Strategy!

This work is a commitment to the many amazing stewards of the world, to share and teach the information, processes and techniques necessary to help you become far more successful. This information will be extremely valuable to those in the healing modalities like the chiropractic, holistic and wellness industries, non-profit organizations, those with a passion for spiritual development and generally people with a purpose and passion greater than their individual wants and desires.

This work also applies to anyone who has a true desire to work better with people and treat them as we all have been instructed through the golden rule - to be treated as you would want and expect to be treated in any situation with respect and dignity. Every interaction we have with people can be enhanced by learning the contents of this book and putting them into action.

The Ideas and techniques we'll discuss are in part pipeline selling which is a long term high quality approach powered by true purpose and passion behind each presentation and interaction. It is an understanding of how the truly successful became that way and ultimately stayed successful no matter the status of the economy, world events or business trends. Every selling great is a people person.

We are all a compellation of the spirit, talent, love and joy with which we surround ourselves. That being said, I have been tremendously blessed over my sales career to be surrounded by some amazing mentors that have shared their secrets and insights to success with me. My commitment for their sharing their insights with me was that I in turn would share what I learned from them with others, along with the extensions or new developments spawned from the implementation of what they taught.

While much of what is contained in "Without Clients" is what I have learned and/or developed from years of face to face selling, there are also many valuable ideas and systems that I will pass along that I have learned from some of the masters. Rest assured, they will be credited where and when it is appropriate for their contributions. They deserve the respect due them for their influence in helping me and many others.

There is a saying that what we resist persists and what we focus on we achieve. All too often, "Heart-Centered" people resist learning how to "sell" in fear that the process might change them, or at the very least how they will be perceived. Instead, let's focus on how to "present from the Heart" by creating an environment for others to say "Yes", and be excited saying it!

We all have been granted infinite capabilities by a Higher Source. It is ultimately up to you to develop and refine those talents in whatever direction your true Heart's desire leads. Learning about and then listening to your personal inner GPS (global positioning satellite) will take you exactly where you want to go once you acknowledge the destination you desire to achieve. Simply put, let your Heart be your guide.

This is a comprehensive program designed to help professional salespeople who sell for a living as well as non-profit staff, patient evaluators and other non-traditional 'salespeople' who sell for survival to create the ideal environment for prospects to buy...

Throughout "Without Clients" you will learn:

- How to further define your purpose and passion
- How and why to accept 100% responsibility for everything in your life
- How to Identify the absolutes of selling
- How to communicate so people want to play with you
- How to identify where Clients are in the buying cycle and how to move them along
- How to make the Cycle of Success work for you
- How to grow life-long relationships with Clients
- How to tackle FEAR head on
- How to get and keep yourself enthusiastically engaged
- How to be the best you can be and be more fulfilled in life

My desire is for you to accomplish everything you desire regarding selling your products, services, goods or representing your offering from the Heartset of who you truly are today.

Collectively, there is so much good we can all accomplish when we team our expertise and put it into action for the right reasons. You and your Heart are an important part of improving our world consistently. Thank you for your efforts on behalf of all you have and will touch positively!

Quote of the Day

"Speakers who talk about what life has taught them never fail to keep the attention of their listeners."
Dale Carnegie

Idea 1: Capture Interest and Attention

Simply put, you have to capture the interest and attention of your prospect. You have to take control by creating, and giving positive energy to the interaction. Remember, you only have one chance to make a first impression!

Here is where enthusiasm comes into play. The expression of its importance was aptly stated by Ralph Waldo Emerson as, "Nothing great was ever achieved without enthusiasm."

As you explore the origin of the word, it takes on even greater meaning. Enthusiasm comes from the Greek, *en theos* or of God's Spirit.

When you have enthusiasm, you are in God's Spirit. You should be having fun! Smile, make eye contact and have positive facial expressions. This is the time for you to capture and to "wow" a prospect.

You need to be genuinely excited, and they need to feel that excitement. Be someone who the prospect wants to be around, and more importantly, wants to listen to.

....

Today's Action Step: Be genuinely enthused as you start your meeting!

....

To learn more, please visit www.ScottSchilling.com

Quote of the Day

"I like to listen. I have learned a great deal from listening carefully. Most people never listen!"
Ernest Hemingway

Idea 2: Be In Tune

You have to "be in tune" with what your prospect needs. I know you'll find this hard to believe, most salespeople typically talk too much. The good Lord was even on our side; He gave us two ears and one mouth. That must mean we're supposed to listen twice as much as we talk.

You have to be in tune; you have to hear what your prospect has to say. Everything you need to know to provide your prospect the best solution to his situation resides within him. He will give you everything you need to know to prepare your presentation if you simply listen.

You also have to be observant of your surroundings and throughout the interaction to notice the clues your prospect is giving off. He will give you everything you need to know to sell him if you pay attention.

Jim Cathcart said it many years ago, "In selling, as in medicine, prescription without diagnosis is malpractice." Being in tune is simply learning and understanding how your prospect is looking to benefit. What is in it for him? Be in tune. You want to accurately assess his needs so that you can solve his issues.

....

Today's Action Step: Have at least 3 probing questions ready to ask your prospect to help you understand his motivation for considering what you have to offer.

....

To learn more, please visit www.ScottSchilling.com

Quote of the Day

"Most of the fundamental ideas of science are essentially simple, and may, as a rule, be expressed in a language comprehensible to everyone."
Albert Einstein

Idea 3: Use Simple Language

So many times, salespeople have the desire to show how much they know; they kind of pound their chest. "I've got this many degrees," "I've done this," "I've done that." You know what the customer says? "I don't care. It's not about you; it's about me.

Relate in a way that I (the prospect) can understand - so use simple language that I can understand."

Many times, especially in the technical professions, salespeople tend to speak technical-ese to their prospect. Be careful in using the language developed around your product or your company. Instead use language that the customer can understand about

31

what your product or your company has to offer and most importantly, how it will benefit him.

If your conversation is blowing you over the top of your client's head, the customer is more than likely not receiving the information he needs to make a decision on your offering.

Also, odds are he is not going to stop you to tell you, because he doesn't want to be embarrassed and admit he doesn't know what you're talking about. Unfortunately, the only way you'll find out is the hard way, when the prospect does not take the action you desire.

....

Today's Action Step: Preview your own presentation to ensure you will be delivering at the prospect's level.

....

To learn more, please visit www.ScottSchilling.com

Quote of the Day

"The wisest have the most authority."
Plato

Idea 4: Be the Authority

People buy from those they perceive to be the authority. Whether you are actually the authority or not, matters less than whether they think you are.

A Heart-Centered seller is going to be the authority because he has a true desire to serve the needs, wants and desires of his prospect.

Many times this is accomplished by front loading the salesperson's effort to become that authority that allows him to truly be an asset to others. How do you become an authority?

You read books; you study; you go to seminars and you listen to programs like this. You do the things that it takes to become better. Perception is larger than fact; you need to go toe-to-toe with the experts. They're the people that you're talking to, because they're the experts on their life.

You need to be the authority on what your product, service or offering is going to do to benefit them in their situation.

....

Today's Action Step: Do a quick recap of your competitor's information prior to your sales call to have his information available at the top of your mind.

....

To learn more, please visit www.ScottSchilling.com

Quote of the Day

"What is it indeed that gives us the feeling of elegance in a solution, in a demonstration?"
Henri Poincare

Idea 5: Demonstrate Your Product

It's often said that a picture is worth 10,000 words! In many cases it is, but there is something even more influential when it comes to presenting a product, good or service if you can do it. What adds power and credibility to your presentation? Demonstrating what you have to offer.

When you are demonstrating, your prospect gets to see whatever it is they are considering in action in their environment. With that, you have to pay close attention and recognize the different learning styles of your prospect: the kinesthetic, the auditory and the visual learners.

Demonstration becomes a great thing for both the kinesthetic,

35

who wants to touch and feel what you have to offer, and the visual learner wants to see what you have to offer. Both tend to get a picture in their minds of your product in action in their setting. The auditory learner wants to hear about all the capabilities and opportunities your offering has to improve their world.

By demonstrating the product, you show them how it works in their situation and they can actually start to take ownership of that product.

....

Today's Action Step: Prepare a demonstration in advance that conveys the value of your offering.

....

To learn more, please visit www.ScottSchilling.com

Quote of the Day

"Men take only their needs into consideration – never their abilities."
Napoleon Bonaparte

Idea 6: Arouse Needs

While we all wished that every prospect recognized his own "needs," many times he simply doesn't. This is where you as the sales professional have to arouse needs of your prospect.

Ultimately, this helps the prospect get on a better track and speeds up the selling cycle by helping him understand some of the needs in his life.

Bottom line, very few people need what they purchase. Rather, they want the benefits that the products, goods or services provide them. Arousing needs is all about creating greater awareness of the prospect's situation.

Some sales trainers suggest finding pain and intensifying it - that's not my style. It's a much more fulfilling relationship when you help the prospect find his "joy," and show him the path to achieve it.

That being said, the fact is people absolutely need certain things. So you want to find out what their needs are; you want to intensify those needs slightly; you want to bring them to a point that you can satisfy those needs through what you have to offer, or potentially other recommendations you can make.

....

Today's Action Step: Research your prospect thoroughly to truly understand what drives him. Once you understand his needs, prioritize them with the help of your prospect and work to provide solid solutions.

....

To learn more, please visit www.ScottSchilling.com

Quote of the Day

> *"A state arises, as I conceive, out of the needs of mankind; no one is self-sufficing, but all of us have many wants."*
> **Plato**

Idea 7: Satisfy Wants

A part of your task as a quality salesperson is to help your prospects understand their wants and deepest desires. By doing that, you then can begin to fulfill their wants by providing the answers they need to accomplish their desires.

You have to create a paradigm shift for the prospect which takes understanding the prospect's original position.

A paradigm quite simply is a set of rules by which your prospects make a decision. In shifting their paradigm, you have to truly understand what they want and are looking to get out of this interaction with you.

39

The prospect knows what he desires; it is up to you to ask enough quality questions to get the information you need to make a presentation that satisfies those wants. Quality questions help qualify the specific wants of your prospect.

Sometimes, it takes work. Not that work is a bad thing; simply do the work; get out in front of it, and by doing that you now have the opportunity to do better.

People want a lot of different things: health, wealth, happiness. Find out what they want and do your best to satisfy them with quality.

....

Today's Action Step: Know your prospect and put yourself in his position to anticipate what he really wants out of this upcoming interaction

....

To learn more, please visit www.ScottSchilling.com

Quote of the Day

"Everything good that I know was taught to me by great teachers and I feel like giving back and sharing the techniques is the thing to do."
Betty Buckley

Idea 8: Discover Shared Views

To create a relationship, you have to be able to share some views with your prospect. His view might be his outlook going forward, or a belief from his past, or even an opinion of what's happening currently.

The more you can gain some type of psychological alignment with him the smoother the sales process will go.

People buy from, associate with, and want to be around those they know, like and trust. To truly know others, you need to share in their world. You have to get them to know you, to like you, and to trust you, and quite frankly, you have to know, like and trust them as well because creating a relationship has to be a two-way street.

One of the best ways to discover common connections is to be observant in the prospect's surroundings. Everything you need to talk with him about in the early stages can be developed around what you notice about and around him.

Sharing in your prospect's outlook promotes growth in a mutual opportunity.

....

Today's Action Step: Find out what is truly of importance to your prospect and talk about that.

....

To learn more, please visit www.ScottSchilling.com

Quote of the Day

"A mind that is stretched by a new experience can never go back to its old dimensions."
Oliver Wendell Holmes, Jr.

Idea 9: Explore Common Experiences

In working together to make this a better planet, you have to share common experiences with others. One of the easiest ways to start the ball rolling is simply be as observant as you possibly can be.

When you go into a person's office, when you go to call on him, pay attention to what's in the office, or what is hanging on the wall, whether there are pictures, or he likes fishing. What are his hobbies? What does he do outside of work? What can you tell from what you observe physically in his surroundings?

Your first goal is to learn as much as you can to create this relationship. This is a relationship that is going to create mutual benefit and success throughout the next number of years. But with that, you want to make sure you do the very best you can to help him get to where he wants to go. This becomes much easier the more you know what makes your prospect tick.

Once you know more, a way to convey this is to share the thought that somebody else just like you had issues like yours, and those issues were solved by their taking this suggested action. It can work for you just like it worked for them. This is the power of the testimonial.

....

Today's Action Step: Become an excellent observer; clues are everywhere: his clothes, his surroundings, and the jewelry he wears. Know the value of what you see.

....

To learn more, please visit www.ScottSchilling.com

Quote of the Day

"It is my feeling that Time ripens all things;
with Time all things are revealed;
Time is the father of truth."
Francois Rabelais

Idea 10: Invest Time

All of us share the exact same 86,400 seconds in a day. If that's true (which it is), why do some people seem to get so much more out of their allotted time? The real answer is that they invest it wisely.

In gaining and growing relationships, you need to invest some time in your prospects. The question becomes, what is your ROI—Return on Investment? This becomes a really important question because time is perishable.

Once that second, minute, hour or day is gone, it's gone forever. Many people agree that time is actually our greatest commodity

45

because unlike anything else, when it's gone it's gone!

It becomes more apparent to me daily (I guess it comes with getting older) that becoming more aware of where we spend our time; and more importantly, what activities we invest it in will truly determine our level of success going forward.

Choose your meetings wisely; qualify your prospects better; and put follow up systems in place to make the most of your investment.

....

Today's Action Step: To ensure the best use of invested time, make certain that you arrive early and only use the committed time. If the interaction may take longer, ask permission to extend your meeting.

....

To learn more, please visit www.ScottSchilling.com

Quote of the Day

"An investment in knowledge pays the best interest."
Benjamin Franklin

Idea 11: Express Interest

People love to be loved. In fact Dr. Gary Chapman has written a great book entitled, "The 5-Love Languages." In his book, Dr. Chapman details how we each have one predominant love language. They are: 1) Words of affirmation; 2) Quality time; 3) Receiving gifts; 4) Acts of service; and 5) Physical touch. As you go through that list, it's not too hard to understand why people respond the way they do based on their language.

Although responding somewhat differently, we all love to have others pay attention to our needs. Your ability to identify and translate your presentation to be consistent with their love language will grow your relationship quickly.

Ultimately you have to show interest in your prospect. You have to understand their situation, because this is what gets you to

47

their appropriate solution. You have to learn about them, their family, their life, their world. You have to empathize in the process; this is about creating a relationship. For greater success, you have to show that interest; they have to feel your Heart. Quite frankly, that's why you're a Heart-Centered salesperson, because you care.

....

Today's Action Step: Think through things that make you feel someone genuinely cares about you and translate similar things into your actions with your prospects.

....

To learn more, please visit www.ScottSchilling.com

Quote of the Day

"No other investment yields as great a return as the investment in education. An educated workforce is the foundation of every community and the future of every economy."

Brad Henry

Idea 12: Share Knowledge

Growing a relationship can be enhanced when you appropriately share knowledge - communicate what you've learned throughout your years of experience from a place of service. You have to understand and communicate the prospect's situation from your frame of reference and understanding to that point. There are few things worse than thinking you're presenting certain information for all the right reasons, yet not having it right.

One key differentiator comes through sharing your knowledge. You can quickly and easily gain authority status by knowing

49

more than just your profession or your product. People expect you to understand your product; what they don't expect is that you know your competition inside and out. Where do you think you get more respect, from knowing your own product, or your competitors?

The answer is - knowing the competition. Every prospect should expect you to know your product, and if they don't, they should. They don't however necessarily expect you to know the other guy's. And when you know the other guy's product, now you've become a true asset, a resource that can be depended upon in any way, shape or form.

....

Today's Action Step: Be a student of your industry, become an expert and trusted resource.

....

To learn more, please visit www.ScottSchilling.com

Quote of the Day

"A pessimist sees the difficulty in every opportunity;
an optimist sees the opportunity in every difficulty!"
Winston Churchill

Idea 13: Remember, Attitude is Everything!

Long ago I heard a Zig Ziglar quote that has played over and over in my head for years. It is "Attitude not Aptitude will determine your Altitude!" In simple words, it's your attitude that will carry you much further than your learned attributes in many cases.

Individually, you think over 50,000 thoughts a day. I'm sure right now there are a few of you asking yourself, "Do I talk to myself? I don't think I talk to myself?"

Because self-talk is programmed into each one of us, positive self-talk is essential. Henry Ford said it back in 1939, "Think you can, think you can't, you're right."

Another one of those famous pieces of self-talk, "I think I can, I think I can" came from the "Little Engine that Could". "I think I can, I think I can, and I think I can." You get plenty of negative influence from the masses on a daily basis. At the very least, you can say nice things to yourself!

You have no idea how much damage you do to yourselves by some of the things that you say. In fact, to the point in which you don't even recognize you say them. Do yourself a favor. Take those 50,000 thoughts a day, and be positive. If it is to be, it's up to me. "Attitude, not Aptitude will determine your Altitude."

....

Today's Action Step: Give yourself a "check up from the neck up" before you enter into any interactions with your prospects.

....

To learn more, please visit www.ScottSchilling.com

Quote of the Day

"Goodwill is the one and only asset that competition cannot undersell or destroy."
Ludwig Borne

Idea 14: Become an Asset

The definition for becoming an asset to one another is simply that of providing value to another person. Following the trick of using acronyms to remember important information, you may want to think of it this way.

An ASSET is being "A Serious Servant Every Time" you can be.

Think about it, if someone you come across was having a miserable day, and you threw them a smile, could it brighten their day a little? You became an asset.

Having the Heartset that you are going to do good for everyone you meet throughout your day puts you in a position to be in the right place at the right time when your prospects are ready to take action. It's all part of "creating an environment to buy."

53

By becoming an asset to others, you create an environment where they naturally gravitate to you and what you have to offer. There is far less selling involved because you have proven to be a trusted resource. As Jim Rohn once said, "If you want to make more money, provide more value!"

....

Today's Action Step: Think through in advance the various ways that you could become an asset to your prospect…and then act on them.

....

To learn more, please visit www.ScottSchilling.com

Quote of the Day

"Efforts and courage are not enough without purpose and direction."
John F. Kennedy

Idea 15: Be "On Purpose"

Why do you do what you do? This is certainly an age old question in man's search for the meaning of life. There are as many answers to this question as you have time to hear. If you are anything like me, the answer has changed significantly over time.

The exciting thing is that with a little exploration and a desire to find your answer, you can find it. (If you need help, go to www.ScottSchilling.com and download the article "Creating a Life Purpose Statement".) What's even better is that after you find it, and then articulate your purpose to your family, friends and anyone you meet, you live it a little more each day.

W. Clement Stone once was quoted, "When you discover your mission, you will feel its demand. It will fill you with enthusiasm and a burning desire to get to work on it."

Purpose is the reason that we individually exist. It is our intended or desired result. Purpose is what gives you your determination and resoluteness. It is the banner you raise and celebrate as you move towards living a fulfilled, happy, healthy and wealthy life.

....

Today's Action Step: Be clear on what truly inspires you. Take a few moments to truly understand your purpose.

....

To learn more, please visit www.ScottSchilling.com

Quote of the Day

"There is no passion to be found in playing small; in settling for a life that is less than the one you are capable of living."
Nelson Mandela

Idea 16: Express Your Passion

So where does passion come from? In most cases, passion is a committed expression of your purpose. It is the enthusiasm that carries you forward. It is the encouragement you need when the going gets tough and you feel like calling it quits. Passion is powerful! It compels you to give everything you've got to pursue the end goal.

Passion is an internal feeling of drive and commitment that shines bright externally. Others feel your passion as you exude the energy behind your desire.

In the book, "Think and Grow Rich," Napoleon Hill talks about passion and enthusiasm as having a burning desire to succeed. He describes it as a state of mind that inspires action.

In fact he goes so far as to say, "Every person who wins in any undertaking must be willing to burn his ships and cut all sources of retreat." Now that's passion!

To express more passion in your personal and professional life, develop that burning desire for the task at hand. Carry it with you and allow it show in everything you do.

....

Today's Action Step: Make sure you are consistently doing what you truly love to do. If not, consider a change...of position...or of attitude toward what you are doing.

....

To learn more, please visit www.ScottSchilling.com

Quote of the Day

"Authentic values are those by which a life can be lived, which can form a people that produce great deeds and thoughts."

Allan Bloom

Idea 17: Be Authentic

We all have been granted infinite capabilities by a Higher Source. It is ultimately up to you to develop and refine those talents in whatever direction your true Heart's desire leads.

Learning about and then listening to your personal inner GPS (global positioning satellite) will take you exactly where you want to go once you acknowledge the destination you desire to achieve. Simply put, let your Heart be your guide.

Dr. Seuss put it this way, "Be who you are and say what you feel because those who mind don't matter and those who matter don't mind!" To be authentic you have to be true to yourself, your principles, and your foundational knowledge. Authenticity is an acceptance or belief resulting from agreement with known facts or experience. It is reliability and trustworthiness. It's a type of wholeness in being and actions.

More importantly, being grounded in purpose and implementing it with passion will take you to levels you have only imagined before.

....

Today's Action Step: Ask five of your closest friends what they see to be your greatest attributes...then play to those strengths because that's more than likely who you really are!

....

To learn more, please visit www.ScottSchilling.com

Quote of the Day

*"The great gift of human beings is that
we have the power of empathy."*
Meryl Streep

Idea 18: Be Empathetic

By definition as noted on dictionary.com, empathy is the intellectual identification with or taking the place of another person or thing; acting or serving as a substitute. Being empathetic is experiencing and relating to the feelings, thoughts, or attitudes of another.

The reason this is so important as a salesperson is simple. There will be many times when you will need to "understand" the position of your prospect from a completely different point of view.

Your ability to empathize with your prospect will actually allow you in many cases to become closer with your prospect because

61

"you care." There are times in everyone's life when they need a shoulder to lean on. The more authentic you are as these situations arise, the more you will be seen as someone who looks past just the dollars and cents of business truly into the Hearts and minds of others.

Master the ability to truly care about others' situations and you will consistently grow your business. People appreciate when you go up and beyond the normal call of business.

....

Today's Action Step: Do your best to be a compassionate listener. Think of how you could be the person who inspires others.

....

To learn more, please visit www.ScottSchilling.com

Quote of the Day

"Compassion brings us to a stop,
and for a moment we rise above ourselves."
Mason Cooley

Idea 19: Show Compassion and Concern

Compassion is an even deeper level of caring for your prospects or Clients. Simply put, it is a feeling of deep sympathy and sorrow for another who is stricken by misfortune. More importantly it is accompanied by a strong desire to alleviate the suffering if at all possible.

When you reach out to those in need, a different level of bond is created between the two of you. When you show concern for another, a higher degree of trust is typically the result.

This can be understood somewhat from Dr. Gary Chapman's 5-Love Languages. People have a desire to feel cared about. How you show it and how they receive it becomes more personal to them. Make sure you do all you can to understand the best way in their eyes for you to show your compassion and concern.

Because of the stronger feeling attached to compassion, it does you good to take more action toward supporting the person or situation you are being compassionate about. There is typically more emotion involved in these interactions and as such, your concern creates a better long term relationship...which is ultimately what you are striving for in the first place.

....

Today's Action Step: Compassion is a genuine desire to feel for another. Self-check to ensure you have the desire to show concern and embrace others.

....

To learn more, please visit www.ScottSchilling.com

Quote of the Day

"A life lived with integrity - even if it lacks the trappings of fame and fortune is a shining star in whose light others may follow in the years to come."
Denis Waitley

Idea 20: Say What You Do and Do What You Say

A number of years ago in one of my trainings, Freddie Rick, the founder of BetterTrades said to his troops, "Your actions speak so loudly I can't hear a word you are saying!" It really impressed upon me the concept of congruency between thought and action.

We live in a society in which people are naturally drawn to those who have already achieved great success. By reviewing this material, you have undoubtedly achieved a greater level than many because you understand the value of consistently improving. The real key is to take that success from a place of

65

confidence as opposed to arrogance.

Arrogance is an inner demon that is unpleasant to be around no matter who you are or what you do. Confidence on the other hand is a certainty in getting the task accomplished with the quality and care it deserves.

State your credentials and commitments truthfully and always make sure that if you say something is going to happen by a certain time, you do everything in your power consistently to meet or exceed expectations.

....

Today's Action Step: Make sure to act with integrity at all times. Do the right thing at the right time for the right reason.

....

To learn more, please visit www.ScottSchilling.com

Quote of the Day

"A style is not a matter of camera angles or fancy footwork; it's an expression, an accurate expression of your particular opinion."

Karel Reisz

Idea 21: Always Be Accurate

Being accurate is simply good form. In any selling situation, you are going to be checked...and checked again to ensure the accuracy of your presentation, your pricing, your delivery schedule, you name it.

Nobody really sets out to be inaccurate. Sometimes it just happens due to lack of communication or information between the parties or within your organization itself.

Do your very best to make sure that you have everything you need to support your case in the best possible light. That does not mean fudge on the facts; in fact make sure you don't.

Prospects and Clients will ask for references from time to time. This happens for a number of reasons. One of the main reasons is to verify and validate the accuracy of your presentation.

If you are ever caught with inaccuracies in what you present, you will be facing an uphill battle going forward. T. Harv Eker addresses this topic extremely well with his quote, "How you do anything is how you do everything." Stick to your principles and be accurate across the board.

....

Today's Action Step: Review all your presentations and support material for their accuracy. Make sure everything is stated with integrity. Also review your competitor's information for its accuracy. Your knowledge allows you to become an asset to your prospects.

....

To learn more, please visit www.ScottSchilling.com

Quote of the Day

"True genius resides in the capacity for evaluation of uncertain, hazardous, and conflicting information."
Winston Churchill

Idea 22: Give Them What They Need to Know

There is a sweet-spot when it comes to the amount of information to share with your prospects and Clients. By sweet-spot I mean the "Goldilocks and the Three Bears" amount; not too much, not too little; just right.

Too many salespeople have the urge to purge and supply every piece of information they have ever learned about their offering.

What is truly needed by the prospect is just enough information to give them the comfort required to make a buying decision. Throughout your presentation, you should be "trial closing" along the way to gauge where your prospect is in the decision making process. A trial close is simply gaining agreement and confirming that the prospect likes where the presentation is, up to this point.

By gaining multiple confirmations along the way, you are both ensuring that they have received what they need in order to make a decision; and that they are tracking along completely with what you are presenting. They need to become comfortable; you need to help them get there.

....

Today's Action Step: When providing information timing is everything, but it is the prospect's timing. Resist over-selling.

....

To learn more, please visit www.ScottSchilling.com

Quote of the Day

*"A dream is your creative vision for
your life in the future. You must break
out of your current comfort zone and become
comfortable with the unfamiliar and the unknown."*
Denis Waitley

Idea 23: Make it Up to Date

It does little or no good to provide information that is dated when talking with your prospects or Clients. We live in an immediate gratification society which among other things has caused people to look at when a piece of information was gathered or produced.

If it is older than perceived to be reasonable, it is discounted or discarded completely.

In fact, if this takes place, you actually stand the chance of losing the prospect altogether, in their eyes. The thought becomes

71

either you don't care or you don't know how to get current information. This then directly relates to your credibility, that of your presentation and offering. Losing credibility because of this type of outside influence is preventable so it makes sense for you to consistently check your sources for their "born-on" dates.

Do the research necessary to ensure your information, presentation and validation are all current and up to date. Ultimately you will reap the rewards of being the most prepared in the eyes of your prospect.

....

Today's Action Step: Subscribe to industry magazines and newsletters to ensure you are up to speed with the latest and greatest your industry has to offer.

....

To learn more, please visit www.ScottSchilling.com

Quote of the Day

"Although our intellect always longs for clarity and certainty, our nature often finds uncertainty fascinating."
Karl Von Clausewitz

Idea 24: Strive for Clarity

One consistent challenge for salespeople is being able to clearly state the benefits their offerings produce because they themselves are actually too close to the product and their company. The old axiom of "you can't see the forest for the trees" comes to mind.

Simply put, because salespeople know everything their offering stands to deliver, they sometimes shortcut the communication process. They get careless describing their offering and as such, the prospect gets confused or at the very least is unclear about the presentation. This creates multiple potential issues.

More than likely, the salesperson is not going to make the sale. The prospect is never going to fess up that he doesn't understand (because he is embarrassed), so the salesperson never receives the feedback to tell him how, what seemed to go so well, went so wrong.

To ensure your message is hitting its target, frequently check with the prospect to gain his comfort level as you proceed. Leave him the opportunity to ask for clarification if and when necessary—you will definitely close more sales.

....

Today's Action Step: Present in such a way to make your prospects feel great about what they are hearing.

....

To learn more, please visit www.ScottSchilling.com

Quote of the Day

"There are people who take rumors and embellish them in a way that can be devastating. And this pollution has to be eradicated by people in our business as best we can."
Bob Woodward

Idea 25: Avoid Over Embellishment

A common pitfall of many a salesperson is their desire to make the product, good or service he is presenting appear to be far superior to what it actually is by over embellishing. Many times embellishment is even used as a failed attempt at humor in the process. In either case, he will lose credibility along the way.

Today especially, we live in an information overloaded world where every little detail you present can be easily scrutinized with the click of a mouse and tapping on a few keys. Virtually any single feature of your offering can be compared within minutes to another potential competitor's offering. Make sure you give your prospects every possible reason to trust you and have absolutely no desire or reasons to even want to compare what you have versus someone else.

You are totally in control of this situation going into your sales presentation. Make sure you display that control and stay positive, above board, and represent your offering with the class and dignity both you and it deserves.

....

Today's Action Step: As they say when you are being sworn in, "Tell the truth, the whole truth and nothing but the truth!"

....

To learn more, please visit www.ScottSchilling.com

Quote of the Day

*"You cannot truly listen to anyone
and do anything else at the same time."*
M. Scott Peck

Idea 26: Listen Carefully

This is going to be a bold statement so I'm making it purposely. Here it goes - "Everything you need to know in order to finalize a sale with your prospect is in his head." He holds all the cards, and it is up to you to be skillful enough to get him to show you his hand.

He will tell you everything you need to know to make this sale happen if and only if you ask enough questions and more importantly, listen carefully to his answers. Think this through.

The prospect is listening to your presentation, and from the minute you start, he is critically evaluating what you are saying about what your offering will do for him. In his mind he is comparing your information to the benefits he perceives and desires to receive.

If you know this to be true, doesn't it make sense to understand what he will be comparing your offering to before you start making the presentation? Ask good quality questions and listen to his answers. He will give you the clues as to what he is looking for and why you can make this the easiest buying decision he has ever made.

....

Today's Action Step: Practice active listening in advance of your interactions with prospects. This is accomplished by hearing everything they have to say, not interrupting and waiting until they conclude to formulate and respond with your answer.

....

To learn more, please visit www.ScottSchilling.com

Quote of the Day

"Criticism may not be agreeable, but it is necessary. It fulfills the same function as pain in the human body. It calls attention to an unhealthy state of things."
Winston Churchill

Idea 27: Accept Criticism Critically

No one likes to hear criticism or negative things coming back at him about his offering—that's human nature. In selling however, many times that criticism will actually hold the key to your ultimate success in selling this prospect.

As a salesperson, if you jump to the defensive, don't hear a prospect out or don't really even give yourself enough time to think through what he is saying, you stand the potential to lose credibility quickly.

The prospect may look at you as simply being over reactive and a non-critical thinker who has a true desire to fulfill his needs above those of the prospect.

As prospects take shots at your offering, or even potentially you personally, hear them out completely. Take time to totally understand their position, clarify what they're saying to ensure you know without a doubt their issue, and then...and only then prepare an answer that professionally addresses their concern.

This is actually a time for you to shine showing understanding, competency and wisdom. Handling criticism with class and responding with dignity can solidify your opportunity going forward.

....

Today's Action Step: Do not jump to the defensive when criticized...stay calm...be professional and be prepared to acknowledge the criticism and respond accordingly.

....

To learn more, please visit www.ScottSchilling.com

Quote of the Day

"Men acquiesce in a thousand things, once righteously and boldly done, to which, if proposed to them in advance, they might find endless objections. "

Robert Dale Owen

Idea 28: Analyze Objections

For years I have trained people to encourage objections. You may be asking yourself, "Why in the world would you want an objection?" The answer is actually quite simple and makes all the sense in the world.

Here it is: "An unspoken objection is still an objection!" Just because it didn't come out doesn't mean it's not there.

At least when an objection comes out, you now know what you are up against. You have a basis to work from. Now you can even start to analyze the objection. Is it real? Is it simply a smokescreen - which is nothing more than a delaying tactic on the part of the prospect. Is it logical? Is it simply a matter of not sharing a critical piece of information for the prospect to be able to make a decision?

The point is you need to answer his objection with quality and that is best accomplished by actually not answering it immediately, but by asking for clarification of why he feels or thinks the way he does.

Once again, the prospect knows what he is really thinking. Your getting defensive or going into over justification mode and working to get him to understand how great your offering is will not work. If it would, he would have already said yes!

....

Today's Action Step: Take time to totally understand a prospect's position. Know your material inside and out. Your knowledge base will then allow you to address any possible concerns after you understand what concerns the prospect truly has.

....

To learn more, please visit www.ScottSchilling.com

Quote of the Day

"Great men are seldom over-scrupulous in the arrangement of their attire."
Charles Dickens

Idea 29: Dress for Success

The old adage, "You only have one chance to make a first impression," is spot on! Whether you like it or not, your appearance casts an image of you from the very first moment someone sets eyes upon you.

You've probably also heard of "love at first sight." That too usually takes place when two people are visually attracted to each other first and foremost.

How you dress says a significant amount about who you are, how you feel and what you think about others.

I say that because when you go around unkempt and possibly not in your Sunday best, you are telling the world "it's more important to me to be comfortable" than it is for me to be dressed appropriately for the setting.

Whether you like it or not, your appearance counts. That includes your physical appearance, grooming, clothes, posture, presence and poise...you name it.

Prospects get a feel for who you are long before you ever get a chance to open your mouth. You can either build credibility or damage it severely by the image you carry. If in doubt, upgrade your attire slightly.

....

Today's Action Step: Be freshly quaffed, look at yourself in the mirror and scan your attire for stains or potential issues. Notice what your prospects will see before meeting them. Be professional!

....

To learn more, please visit www.ScottSchilling.com

Quote of the Day

"All credibility, all good conscience, all evidence of truth come only from the senses."
Friedrich Nietzsche

Idea 30: Establish Credibility

To be credible, you must be worthy of belief or confidence; you must be trustworthy. This comes back to one of the absolutes taught earlier; people buy from those they know, like and trust.

Prospects want to do business with people that are like them, a salesperson that they have grown to like, a salesperson who has shown his skills in solving a problem that prospect needed to be solved. Prospects look to do business with someone who can demonstrate his expertise to the advantage of the prospect.

Because credibility is about trustworthiness, one of the easiest ways to grow your credibility is to accept responsibility for everything that happens in your life. By definition, responsibility is the ability to respond. Your ability to respond in all situations with class and dignity will go a long way in establishing your credibility as a trusted resource with whom people want to be around and do business. Your word is your bond and a hand shake is a hand shake. Make them count.

....

Today's Action Step: Credibility and trust are earned attributes. Know that going in and understand that it is your responsibility to earn your position and credibility.

....

To learn more, please visit www.ScottSchilling.com

Quote of the Day

"Only a life lived for others is a life worthwhile."
Albert Einstein

Idea 31: Speak from Their Orientation

You can differentiate yourself quickly and easily as a quality salesperson with one simple positioning action made from the very minute you first meet your prospect. It comes from a thought process of WIIFT...What's In It For Them?

Come from a place of others' orientation. In today's terms this position is called, "Servant Leadership".

Servant leadership is a philosophy and practice of leadership coined and defined by Robert Greenleaf in the 1970's that is even far more prevalent and applicable in today's sales environment.

This viewpoint comes from a place of providing a solution and not simply having a desire to sell something.

In order to be a servant leader, one needs the following qualities: listening, empathy, healing, awareness, persuasion, conceptualization, foresight, stewardship, growth and the ability to build community. Acquiring these qualities tend to give a person authority versus power.

Today we live in a society where becoming an asset to all you come across and providing good sound solutions to the needs of others is what will launch your business to greater success.

....

Today's Action Step: Put yourself in your prospect's position. You'll sell far more and faster than you ever imagined. Be genuine and sincere in understanding what he needs and his position.

....

To learn more, please visit www.ScottSchilling.com

Quote of the Day

"Your purpose is to make your audience see what you saw, hear what you heard, feel what you felt. Relevant detail, couched in concrete, colorful language, is the best way to recreate the incident as it happened and to picture it for the audience."
Dale Carnegie

Idea 32: Know Your Audience

How well do you know your prospect before you ever make your first sales call? If the answer is not all that well, you might want to reconsider your approach. To be a quality salesperson, you have to be a step ahead of the game.

The reason is simple, because of the quantity of information that is available to your prospect at the drop of the hat, he knows plenty about you, your organization, your offering; and more importantly, your competition than you can imagine.

You have a great opportunity today to provide tremendous value to those you serve by learning as much about them, their potential issues, their buying process; and your competition who may just be able to also satisfy their needs, wants and desires instead of you.

Understanding your audience is key to a quality presentation and therefore solution. Do as much research as possible to know as much as you can about the organization, people, culture, style and business model as you can.

Your prospect has honored you by granting you a meeting; now you return that honor by providing them massive value in your solution.

....

Today's Action Step: Research, research, research! Know as much as you can about your prospect prior to getting face to face.

....

To learn more, please visit www.ScottSchilling.com

Quote of the Day

*"You cannot open a book
without learning something."*
Confucius

Idea 33: Learn Their Mode of Receiving Information

If you want to connect more closely with your prospects, one great way to leap ahead of the crowd is to identify and understand your prospect's dominate learning modality. Everyone takes in information and learns based upon his personalized receptor system.

We all have the standard five senses: smell, taste, sight, touch and sound. In actuality, we all have a sixth sense as well called intuition, or as some call it, a "gut feeling."

According to a Diablo Valley College, California, study, these senses become refined into four specific learning styles. When learned by a sales professional, these styles can be used to present more effectively and ultimately grow your business. The reason for your impending success is simple; you will now have the ability to deliver the information necessary to make a buying decision in the best mode for your prospect to receive it.

The Visual/Verbal learning style learns best when information is presented visually and through the written word. The Visual/Nonverbal learning style learns best when information is presented visually and in a picture or design. The Auditory/Verbal learning style learns best when information is presented verbally through the spoken word, and the Feeling/Kinesthetic learning style learns best when physically engaged in a "hands on" activity.

....

Today's Action Step: Take a few moments to understand your own learning style, and then practice by studying those around you to understand their personal style.

....

To learn more, please visit www.ScottSchilling.com

Quote of the Day

"The only thing worse than being blind is having sight but no vision."
Helen Keller

Idea 34: Help the Visual See

There are two types of visual learners. The first are visual/verbal and the second are visual/non-verbal. To ensure that you are the most effective you can possibly be with your presentations, it is best to know the subtle differences between the two.

Let's first address the visual/verbal learner. He learns best when information is presented visually and through the written word. Your prospect will absorb the most information when you present using a white board or PowerPoint presentation that uses bullet points to frame your presentation.

He loves to read support material after the fact. He will often review information by re-reading it in his "mind's eye."

The second visual learner is a visual/non-verbal combination. He learns best when your information is presented visually and in a picture or design. To reach this modality effectively, you will want to use visual aids, charts, graphs and anything that can help him picture your offering in action. He will often review information by seeing a picture in his mind.

Studies suggest that as much as 65% of people are visual learners. Helping your prospects "see" the benefits your offering delivers will increase your success rate significantly.

....

Today's Action Step: Create visual aids, PowerPoint presentations, and flip charts that address both the verbal and non-verbal tendencies of your prospects to accurately present in the style that will be received the best.

....

To learn more, please visit www.ScottSchilling.com

Quote of the Day

"If I was hearing something I couldn't do,
I would figure out how to do it."
Bill Bruford

Idea 35: Help the Auditory Hear

The auditory/verbal learner comprehends best when information is presented verbally through the spoken word. This type of prospect learns best by listening to your presentation and then creating a group discussion about the subject matter. Very often he will benefit from listening to a recorded version of your presentation to support what he has already heard.

When an auditory learner remembers something, he will playback the conversation and "hear" your words again.

Understanding this process becomes important because the quality of your voice and diction come into play. If you do not speak clearly, the message tends to get lost because of the medium.

If your prospect fits into this learning category, you are best served by creating a group dynamic in which significant discussion can be created around the benefits of your offering.

Other key ingredients to success include regulating your voice tone, inflection, and body language. Doing these things will help your prospects maintain interest and attention. Auditory prospects take the action you are requesting when information is presented and requested verbally.

....

Today's Action Step: Make sure you talk clearly and succinctly when addressing an auditory learning prospect.

....

To learn more, please visit www.ScottSchilling.com

Quote of the Day

*"It's often just enough to be with someone.
I don't need to touch them. Not even talk. A feeling
passes between you both. You're not alone."*
Marilyn Monroe

Idea 36: Help the Kinesthetic Feel

The feeling/kinesthetic learner comprehends best when physically engaged in a "hands on" activity. The kinesthetic wants to really be part of the demonstration of your offering. He needs to "feel" what you're presenting both figuratively and literally. If you have a product you can put into their hands...do it.

If there is a chance of your prospect assembling something that represents your offering, he will dive in whole-Heartedly. You could use a model to illustrate a concept, or provide a site inspection to show the level of quality and/or dependability of what you are offering.

The bottom line is pretty simple; if he can touch it he can trust it.

The other side to the kinesthetic is the intuitive side. Many times this type of prospect is tuned into his ability to give and take energy and with that, he has an uncanny ability to perceive things with a "gut feeling" sensation.

....

Today's Action Step: Make sure you are absolutely compatible with how you feel and the energy you give off when presenting to kinesthetic learners.

....

To learn more, please visit www.ScottSchilling.com

Quote of the Day

*"Judge a man by his questions
rather than his answers."*
Voltaire

Idea 37: Ask Questions to Truly Understand

To make any selling situation easier, there is one simple idea that will make your efforts go farther and allow you to achieve more than you ever dreamed possible. The key is to learn to ask quality questions of your prospect. He knows every reason why he will buy and also every reason that will keep him from buying.

Doesn't it make sense that when you know this to be true, you might as well go ahead and ask him to find out?

Start with no pre-conceived destination in mind, meaning allow the questions to lead to wherever the prospect takes you. You are not working to pin your prospect into a corner rather you are working to allow him to tell you what you need to satisfy in his mind for him to say yes.

Next begin the process of "active listening." Ask a question and carefully listen to the answer. Select a word, concept or phrase from the answer and create a new question to ask. Then repeat, and repeat, and repeat.

When you do this, he will ultimately divulge what is truly important to him which now gives you the opportunity to tailor your presentations to the prospect's needs, wants and desires.

....

Today's Action Step: Practice active questioning and listening with a co-worker, spouse or simply anyone you meet. You'll be amazed at how much information they will give you when you allow them to determine the path.

....

To learn more, please visit www.ScottSchilling.com

Quote of the Day

"A creative man is motivated by the desire to achieve, not by the desire to beat others."
Ayn Rand

Idea 38: Learn Their Motivations

Each prospect takes action directly because of some benefit he will receive for doing so. People act for selfish reasons. Quite frankly, that's okay. When you know those reasons, you can better understand how to present your offering in a way that solves his issue.

The two prime foundation motivators are that people flee from pain and strive for pleasure. Unfortunately most sales trainers will encourage you to identify the prospects pain and intensify it - kind of pick at the scab. Just the metaphor sounds gross, so why would you want to do that?

Your desire is for a long term relationship. Ask yourself one simple question, would you like someone to do that to you? Of course not...so why would you do it to anyone else? It may allow you to get a quick sale...but never allow you to create a relationship and get their repeat business.

Find out the pleasure that your prospects would like to achieve. Help them reach their goal and achieve that pleasurable result through the benefits provided by your offering. When you have accomplished that, you have made the sale, created a repeat buyer, and more than likely a friend along the way!

....

Today's Action Step: Go ahead and look for what motivates people, especially the good they want to achieve. Ask a few people, "What would a perfect situation look like to you?" You'll be amazed at the vision they will share.

....

To learn more, please visit www.ScottSchilling.com

Quote of the Day

"There is only one class in the community that thinks more about money than the rich, and that is the poor. The poor can think of nothing else."
Oscar Wilde

Idea 39: Focus on Money When Dollars Matter

Throughout your selling career, you will come across a number of prospects who are ultimately motivated by the all-mighty dollar. While this may or may not be what totally motivates you, your motivations are not nearly as important as the motivations of your prospect.

It's really not too hard to identify those who have a "profit" motive. These are the prospects that strive for success through money, possessions, acquisitions, wealth, income and growth. You should be able to spot them freely by the cars they drive, watches they wear, places they frequent, and grandiose vision

103

they project.

There is no judgment here. If possessions drive them to succeed, so be it. Simply understand their desires and also how to incorporate more of the above into the presentation of what you have to offer.

Those prospects who are driven by the dollar need to feel that they will personally profit significantly by saying "Yes" to your offering. If they do not feel that personal reward, they will find a supplier that provides a similar offering and who will provide them the personal reward they desire.

....

Today's Action Step: Set a plan into action to determine exactly how much is enough when it comes to a prospect's definition of personal reward.

....

To learn more, please visit www.ScottSchilling.com

Quote of the Day

"Congratulations. I knew the record would stand until it was broken."
Yogi Berra

Idea 40: Focus on Public Acknowledgement When Recognition Matters

Throughout your selling career, you will come across a number of prospects who are ultimately motivated by being recognized for the job they do. While recognition may not be your motivator, keep in mind it may be important to your prospect.

Prospects who are motivated by "recognition" are craving respect, admiration, regard, notoriety, esteem and celebrity. They have a true desire to be "known" for the solution "they" found to the company's issue. In and of itself, this is not an issue. How you handle it could be.

This type of buyer needs to feel as if they are on top of the world for providing the solution. Knowing that, do your best to allow them to take the credit for the decision, and also help spread the word, obviously within reason, throughout their system and the industry. Notoriety is important so help them "get their 15 minutes of fame".

....

Today's Action Step: Let your prospect take credit for success. Share news of his "great decision" as is appropriate within the corporate structure.

....

To learn more, please visit www.ScottSchilling.com

Quote of the Day

"Anyone who acquires more than the usual amount of knowledge concerning a subject; is bound to leave it as his contribution to the knowledge of the world."

Liberty Hyde Bailey

Idea 41: Focus on Contribution When Legacy Matters

Throughout your selling career, you will come across a number of prospects who are ultimately motivated by the contributions they have made and the legacy they have left for the job they have done. Although legacy may not be a motivator for you, remember it may be significant to your prospect.

This type of prospect is motivated internally - from the Heart. He is committed to his morals, duty, honor and philanthropy. Doing the right thing for the right reason at the right time is very important to this prospect.

With this type of prospect the presentation of your offering should take on the position of what this decision will do for others far beyond the scope of the normal offering. This prospect is driven by the legacy he has created. Therefore present day considerations are far less important than long term effects.

Show your prospect how making the decision to purchase your offering is consistent with his desire to make a contribution to the greater good, and the deal is yours!

....

Today's Action Step: Make sure you build into your offering a natural victory for your prospect so he can feel great about his decision.

....

To learn more, please visit www.ScottSchilling.com

Quote of the Day

"To enjoy good health, to bring true happiness to one's family, to bring peace to all, one must first discipline and control one's own mind. If a man can control his mind he can find the way to Enlightenment, and all wisdom and virtue will naturally come to him."

Buddha

Idea 42: Focus on Family When Family Matters

Throughout your selling career, you will come across a number of prospects who are ultimately motivated by their desire to provide for their families and enjoy as much time with them as possible. While family life may not a motivator for you, your motivations are not nearly as important as the motivations of your prospect.

This type of prospect has worked to develop a balance in life which allows him to accomplish his professional goals while still

109

being able to spend time with and nurture his family. Knowing this he is not going to be pushed into deadlines or situations that interfere with family matters. Because family is of such importance, anything that you can do to represent your offering in such a way to make the transaction go smoothly, enabling him to maintain his family schedule is a plus.

Another important approach with this prospect is to include the importance of family into your presentation if at all possible. Beyond every work situation there are always family matters on both sides. Sharing information about your family and their importance to you as your support system will go a long way toward creating a solid working relationship with your prospect.

....

Today's Action Step: Learn as much about your prospect's family, hobbies, favorite activities, and what makes their "togetherness" so important to them prior to your interactions to create a foundational talking point.

....

To learn more, please visit www.ScottSchilling.com

Quote of the Day

"Just as your car runs more smoothly and requires less energy to go faster and farther when the wheels are in perfect alignment, you perform better when your thoughts, feelings, emotions, goals, and values are in balance."

Brian Tracy

Idea 43: Make Sure to Sell Dog Food to Dogs

One of the most common mistakes being made by sales professionals for years has been attempting to sell the wrong product to the wrong prospect. It doesn't seem like that would be possible, but it happens all the time.

The way it starts typically is when the salesperson doesn't do enough research and assumes the prospect has a need or even a desire for what he has to offer, when in fact he doesn't.

111

The key word is "assume"...but he really doesn't know for sure. It also happens because a salesperson will take a shotgun approach to prospecting meaning he throws a large swatch of information out to the masses hoping to connect with somebody who wants what he has to offer. This type of diffused prospecting may find a client here or there from time to time, but it will be a very inefficient approach in the long run.

You are far better to have a targeted approach, more like that of a rifle. You will be far more accurate, waste less time and accomplish more because you have refined your search for prospects before you started presenting to those who have no desire to hear what you have to say.

....

Today's Action Step: Research your prospects thoroughly. Know who your offering applies to in advance of making your presentation. Develop the ability to quickly spot those who have a need and desire for what you have to offer.

....

To learn more, please visit www.ScottSchilling.com

Quote of the Day

"A wise woman puts a grain of sugar into everything she says to a man, and takes a grain of salt with everything he says to her."

Helen Rowland

Idea 44: Give a Spoon Full of Sugar...

When you are living in a selling environment day in and day out, some things are not going to happen just exactly as planned.

Both you and your prospect had every intention of everything working out perfectly and then somewhere along the way stuff happens. And usually when stuff happens, someone isn't too pleased about it.

This is the time to remember that ultimately you are working to create a long term relationship with this prospect, and if you want it to be positive, you may have to subordinate your emotions in addressing the issue. Notice, this approach does not say compromise your integrity, or give away the store, it simply says maintain a desire to create a solution to the problem.

When delivering the solution, look for the positives that have come out of the issue. There are always lessons to be learned when you look for them. Once you identify that potential lesson, use it to soften the blow of the issue...you know, the old "a spoon full of sugar helps the medicine go down" approach.

Make your solution as palatable as possible for both you and your prospect.

....

Today's Action Step: Research well in advance how to best present a compromise or address a potentially fatal situation that could kill a deal. Anticipating a situation in advance and being prepared to handle it properly demonstrates your desire to be a professional.

....

To learn more, please visit www.ScottSchilling.com

Quote of the Day

"We know the past and its great events, the present in its multitudinous complications, chiefly through faith in the testimony of others."
Matthew Simpson

Idea 45: Obtain a Strong Third Party Testimonial

Third party testimonials about you, your offering and your organization are always far stronger than the exact same information you tell the prospect yourself. The reason is simple, your prospect expects you to tell him that you are the best rep, your offering is the best available, and your company is second to none.

In fact if you don't tell him all of that, he'll probably be wondering if you really believe it yourself.

The most efficient way to get positive points across about how good you, your offering and your company are, is to have a trusted source give a testimonial on your behalf. By trusted source I mean someone who the prospect trusts, someone who is like them within another organization, an individual with a recognized public persona, or some type of industry expert in the same field.

The concept is simple; this trusted source has had great success, a wonderful relationship, or some very positive interaction with you and your offering. The prospect can now see himself enjoying those same positive attributes with you going forward.

....

Today's Action Step: Before making your sales call, establish who would give the most powerful and influential testimonial for your product to the particular prospect you will be calling on.

....

To learn more, please visit www.ScottSchilling.com

Quote of the Day

"I have expertise in five different fields which helps me to easily understand the analogy between my scientific problems and those occurring in nature."
Philip Emeagwali

Idea 46: Be Confident in Your Expertise

No matter where you are in your evolution as a sales person, you have achieved a level of expertise unlike any other because it is yours. You are the best "you" out there, and as such you should rise to the level of your accomplishments. By no way am I suggesting that you should become arrogant. Rather, I am suggesting is that you remain confident in your accomplishments to date and have a desire for constant and never-ending personal improvement.

Position yourself as an expert in your field. The reason is simple; people do not question the recommendations of experts. Think about it. You don't question a brain surgeon, an accountant or even your auto repairman because they have knowledge about their area of expertise that their prospect does not.

Remember, perception of being an authority in many cases is sufficient. Be a student of your industry and know your offering and systems inside out. When you establish credibility, prospects will typically not challenge it.

....

Today's Action Step: Practice projecting your confidence by talking about the area in which you are absolutely the best. For example, you may be a great downhill skier. Talk to someone about skiing (a subject you have down cold) and reflect on how you feel as you talk with confidence. Then transfer that same feeling over to your presentations.

....

To learn more, please visit www.ScottSchilling.com

Quote of the Day

"All things entail rising and falling timing.
You must be able to discern this."
Miyamoto Musashi

Idea 47: Understand Their Timing!

The third absolute in presenting anything is that your prospect will take action - when they are ready. It has nothing to do with when you want them to commit, or how long you have been working this deal. It has everything to do with the prospect's desire to solve his issues on his time frame.

He wants to know how your offering will benefit him. Then when he is comfortable that he knows you, likes you and trusts you, he will take action.

Knowing this, it makes sense in the early stages of your learning about what your prospect needs to ask a very simple yet often forgotten question. It is, "Provided you like everything you see and hear about our offering, when will you be making the decision to purchase?" Another way is a little more roundabout with, "Once you have explored all your options, when will you need the offering delivered?"

In either case, you now have a gauge as to how long a decision will take, how many other offerings other than yours the prospect may be looking at, and when he wants the offering to be in place. Through two simple questions you have obtained some very critical information.

....

Today's Action Step: Study the two questions in this lesson and make sure you can deliver them with total comfort.

....

To learn more, please visit www.ScottSchilling.com

Quote of the Day

"A man cannot be comfortable without his own approval."
Mark Twain

Idea 48: Make Your Surroundings Professional

Because there are so many virtual companies and environments these days, there are times when you as the salesperson can have control of the location where you will be meeting. If that is the case, make sure you choose a location that is conducive to the business about to be conducted.

While so many people love Starbucks today and there are plenty of meetings that can be held there with quality, there are also plenty that cannot.

Too often salespeople get into a rut of staking a claim in a place that is comfortable for them but is not necessarily comfortable for their prospect and worse yet, not really appropriate for

121

doing business.

Much like "up-grading" your attire to create a solid impression, meeting locations and the comfort and privacy they afford can accomplish the same thing. There are some great social clubs, executive suites or even hotel environments that can add some class and ambiance to your meeting.

Most importantly, you want to be in a location that allows for quality communications between you and your prospect.

....

Today's Action Step: Find a location that is congruent with the nature of your business and the quality of your offering far before you need it.

....

To learn more, please visit www.ScottSchilling.com

Quote of the Day

*"In order to be irreplaceable
one must always be different."*
Coco Chanel

Idea 49: Present Last When Possible

In many selling situations, you will not be the only person to present a potential solution to your prospect. If this is in fact the case, do your best to be the last salesperson to present to the prospect and decision maker.

The reason is simple. As your prospect is inundated with multiple sets of information and things to consider, he will undoubtedly begin to somewhat "numb-out" meaning his senses and memories may become over-loaded.

Ideally, you want the last thing on his mind to be your offering and all the wonderful benefits you will be delivering. Your offering will be at the top of his mind when you go into the consideration phase.

Another reason for presenting last is that your prospect will have assimilated all the other information he has gathered prior to your presentation. The prospect will have a better idea of what questions need to be asked because he will have the information to make comparisons.

This gives you a great advantage because those who presented before you will not have the opportunity to answer key questions that will ultimately lead to a buying decision. Advantage you!

....

Today's Action Step: Make it a habit to know how many presentations your prospect will be seeing and who they will be from. Work to be the last one he sees.

....

To learn more, please visit www.ScottSchilling.com

Quote of the Day

"Insanity: doing the same thing over and over again and expecting different results."
Albert Einstein

Idea 50: Focus on the Ideal Result

Just like when prospecting, far too many salespeople go into a presentation with a shotgun approach. They are willing to take any little bit of success in hoping that the prospect will continue to want more from them over time. While that may work sometimes, it does not work nearly as well as going in with a solid plan and a primary objective.

Focus your efforts on your primary objective. Make sure you do not dilute your efforts by bringing up all sorts of ancillary goals with the potential of confusing the prospect. Stay on point to ensure you gain agreement from your prospect.

The only time to bring in a secondary objective is well after all the details regarding your primary objective have been put to bed. One of the major mistakes salespeople make is over-selling or selling themselves out of a deal. In other words, gaining agreement on the primary objective is all that was needed to secure the deal but because additional information was provided, other questions were raised that put the first agreement into jeopardy.

Secure the deal at hand and make sure you have everything you need to deliver.

....

Today's Action Step: Have a plan for what you are going to present and stay the course in presenting it.

....

To learn more, please visit www.ScottSchilling.com

Quote of the Day

"The creation of a thousand forests is in one acorn."
Ralph Waldo Emerson

Idea 51: Co-create with Your Prospect Whenever Possible

Prospects are much more likely to accept and promote solutions they have a hand in producing. If you want to rally support of your offering, ask your prospect to supply input regarding how to make your presentation the most effective for his group. The time to gather this support is prior to any major presentation to a multi-person, decision making group.

Many times you can identify a champion in the organization who can lend you keen insight into the decision making process of his organization. How can you make your presentation more "user-friendly" in nature? Are there any corporate cultural issues with which you can align, to give your presentation a more "homespun" feel?

If you have any indication that there may be opposition to any parts of your presentation, seek out what those points might be in advance and establish a strategy for addressing them well in advance of your interaction.

The simple fact is when prospects participate in creating the solution, you have made great strides in winning the approval of all involved.

....

Today's Action Step: Find an ally from the group setting who can help you tailor your presentation for greater success.

....

To learn more, please visit www.ScottSchilling.com

Quote of the Day

"To be, or not to be: that is the question."
William Shakespeare

Idea 52: Ask Specific Questions to Get Specific Answers

There is an old adage when it comes to asking questions in a sales environment. It is simply, the better the quality of your questions, the better the quality the answers will be.

Many times salespeople open themselves up for long, drawn-out answers because they initiated them by asking a far too general question.

For example if you ask, "What's going on with your business?" the possible answers are almost limitless.

There are a couple inherent problems with this approach. First, it's a time waster for all concerned because the person answering the questions doesn't know what part of his business to tell you about. Second, as the salesperson, you more than likely will not get the specific information you desire.

On top of that, you chewed up some valuable time without really accomplishing anything. Become an asset and help guide the prospect to reveal important facts for making a positive buying decision later on.

....

Today's Action Step: Design and ask precise, targeted questions that get you the information you need to craft your presentation accordingly.

....

To learn more, please visit www.ScottSchilling.com

Quote of the Day

"I think if you get asked to do this, then that's called doing your homework, and I try and do it."
Mark Harmon

Idea 53: Do Your Homework. Make Sure Others Do Too!

Being a student of your industry takes you far beyond the scope of most salespeople. To become a sales professional, you have to go up and beyond the call of duty. At the very least you have to know your offering. Some may think that's simplistic, but unfortunately so many so-called sales people don't.

The next level takes not only knowing your offering, but the offerings of your competitors as well. Prospects will use any advantage they can in hammering out the best deal possible for them and their organization. If they have greater knowledge and understanding than you of what is offered, they will definitely use it to potentially compromise your offering. That's

131

their job.

Your job is equally as important, to present and defend the honor and pricing of your offering. Typically in this case, the person with the most knowledge prevails.

There is another reason to do as much research as you possibly can. It is because with additional knowledge you have the ability to become far more valuable as a resource to your prospect. He can now draw upon your knowledge to assist him with achieving your common goal - buying your offering.

....

Today's Action Step: Strive to learn at least one thing about your competition or industry every day.

....

To learn more, please visit www.ScottSchilling.com

Quote of the Day

"The wise ones fashioned speech with their thought, sifting it as grain is sifted through a sieve."
Buddha

Idea 54: Vary Your Pacing and Intensity

Studies show that a person can listen and absorb information six times faster than most people talk. It's not hard to understand why a person's average attention span is about 5 to 6 minutes before they start to drift away.

The brain is moving far faster than the information is being delivered. One easy idea to maintain attention is to vary the pace of your speaking.

If you see your prospects starting to drift off inadvertently, increase your pace to re-capture their attention. You obviously don't want to make it so fast that it affects your pronunciation and diction, but you do want to make a purposeful shift to pull the prospect back in.

Another vocal tactic to capture your audience comes with varying the intensity with which you deliver the message. Being able to present and vary your intensity will allow you to convey a different level of passion in your presentation.

Similar to pacing, too much intensity has diminishing returns as well. You can't start out at a fevered pitch if you plan on showing more intensity later on. Being too intense will have a counter effect on what you want to convey.

....

Today's Action Step: Practice modifying your pace and intensity with a co-worker to understand the timing of your modifications and the effects they deliver.

....

To learn more, please visit www.ScottSchilling.com

Quote of the Day

*"Inspiration is enough to give expression
to the tone in singing, especially when
the song is without words."*
Franz Liszt

Idea 55: Vary Your Tone and Inflection

Professor Albert Mehrabian conducted an intensive study of non-verbal communications at UCLA. As it applied to feelings and attitudes throughout the communications process, Mehrabian concluded that 7% of the meaning came through the words, 38% of the meaning came through the tonality with which they were delivered, and 55% of the meaning came through physiology or expressions.

The reason this is so important to understand in the selling situation is because words convey more "meaning" than the words themselves.

In fact, the tone in which you deliver the words can greatly increase or decrease the reception of and meaning attached to the words.

As a professional salesperson, you need to learn how to make words "dance" by changing your tone and inflection as you deliver them. You can say "that's great" in an unemotional, drab delivery or say the exact same words with an excited tone and inflection, and change the way the words are interpreted.

The important thing to remember is that tone and inflection dictate the true meaning attached to the words.

....

Today's Action Step: Make sure your tone and inflection are congruent with the meaning of the words you are saying to get your point across.

....

To learn more, please visit www.ScottSchilling.com

Quote of the Day

"Discontent is the first necessity of progress."
Thomas A. Edison

Idea 56: Embrace Positive Discontent vs. Dissatisfaction

Contentment is a wonderful thing but so is what I call a "positive discontent." Contentment can actually be the enemy of living your life to its fullest. A long time ago someone shared the saying, "You are either green and growing or ripe and rotting." Who wants to be rotting? Stagnation is a terrible thing.

My realization of positive discontent came out of a mastermind group where a friend was sharing his ten rules to live by. One of his rules was "never be satisfied." Immediately my gut fired a message to my brain, "Oh, what a shame. How do you enjoy life if you are never satisfied?" Then my intuition kicked in. How about re-languaging the concept in a more positive and applicable way? What came to mind was Positive Discontent.

Although you won't find it in Webster's dictionary, here is the definition I developed. Positive discontent is a process by which you have total and unapologetic gratitude for everything in your life. Yet you hold the accompanying positive expectation that a Higher Source and the universe has even more great things in store for you.

Positive discontent is the inner voice that helps you strive to the next level, whatever that may mean to you. It's the part of you that keeps you growing for the greater good.

....

Today's Action Step: Be grateful for everything that is going on in your career. At the same time, consistently take a critical look at what areas you can improve and take action toward.

....

To learn more, please visit www.ScottSchilling.com

Quote of the Day

"A great trademark is appropriate, dynamic, distinctive, memorable and unique."

Primo Angeli

Idea 57: Learn What Makes You Unique

What are your Unique Selling Propositions (USPs)? They are the attributes that differentiate you from your competition who offer similar products, goods or services. It is imperative that you determine what makes you different from the rest. It is these USPs that become the strong hold for you to establish your sales and marketing efforts around.

There are typically five traits that give companies superiority over others. I want to thank my friend Phil Town for sharing this with me and ultimately with you. The traits include:

Brand – A name that is known and respected so much that a prospect will purchase it over others because he trusts what he will get. Coke and McDonald's would be Brand examples.

Secret - A trade secret, patent or proprietary nature which differentiates the offering. Examples include formulas owned by 3M, Merck, and Pfizer.

Toll - Control of the marketplace such that any business that comes through it must in essence "pay a toll" to play in that industry. The large media companies and utilities, prior to deregulation, fit this category.

Switching - Offerings that are so elaborate it becomes too costly or too consuming to switch away from them. Offerings including the products of Microsoft, ADP or Paychex are examples.

Low Cost - Offerings priced so low others cannot compete. In this category you could name products from Walmart, Costco and Target as examples.

One easy way to determine your USPs is to look at your competitors' advertising and marketing efforts. What are they saying to compete against you? This information will give you their thoughts on what they believe to be unique about them.

....

Today's Action Step: Take a few moments to sit down and really think through these questions: "What is it about you personally, professionally or socially that gives you an advantage over everyone else?" and "What are they targeting to compete against you?" Once you compile your USPs, incorporate them into your sales presentation.

Quote of the Day

*"Personality is only ripe when a man
has made the truth his own."*
Soren Kierkegaard

Idea 58: Know Your Personality Type

There have been many studies throughout the years as well as educational systems put into place to help salespeople understand the four basic personality types of prospects. You may have heard of the DISC profile which rates people according to Dominance, Influence, Steadiness, and Conscientiousness.

Because people think in pictures, I choose to train them using animals to represent the four categories. I learned this technique from Steve Scott. It seems easy to simply picture an animal and then relate to its behavior, because a person more than likely already has a life-long understanding of its tendencies. These choices are ultimately consistent with DISC, or any of the others to which a person may have been exposed.

The four categories are Lions, Otters, Golden Retrievers and Beavers. The Lion has a fast paced, task orientation. The Otter has a fast paced, people orientation. The Golden Retriever has a slow paced, people orientation. The Beaver has a slow paced, task orientation.

The reason for knowing this information is simple, a Golden Retriever presenting to a Lion without knowing they're a Lion will get swallowed up. A playful Otter presenting to a Beaver will frustrate the heck out of them.

In most cases, salespeople will be Otters because of their creativity, playfulness, influence and love for interaction with others. Learn your type, and then the meanings behind the other types and you will be more successful.

....

Today's Action Step: Go to **www.ScottSchilling.com** and down load the article entitled, "Why Knowing Your Personality Type is Important." Take the test included to determine your type.

....

To learn more, please visit www.ScottSchilling.com

Quote of the Day

"A truly strong person does not need the approval of others any more than a lion needs the approval of sheep."
Vernon Howard

Idea 59: Learn How To Present to a Lion Personality

The Lion is the king of the jungle, at least certainly in its mind. This personality type makes up about 15% of the population. He is a power player who is typically motivated by money and challenge. He is said to be a workaholic, is very focused and doesn't play around. He is not into hugs and feelings.

Lions are typically the controllers, CEOs and presidents of companies. They are the leaders of organizations, fast paced and task oriented. They are typically very productive, have big egos and like to walk over people.

143

The keys to presenting to a Lion are as follows. He believes he is of ultimate importance so you must absolutely show your respect. Because of the pace and task orientation, you need to get down to business and stick to it. Stay on point.

You'll want to present briskly, because if you're too slow or long and drawn out, the Lion will sense incompetence. And if you are a Lion yourself, you stand the potential of fighting for dominance. You have to find common ground and agree to work together to make things happen.

....

Today's Action Step: When presenting to a Lion, make sure your presentation is highly organized, that you have all the facts and are prepared by anticipating challenges along the way.

....

To learn more, please visit www.ScottSchilling.com

Quote of the Day

"Just play. Have fun. Enjoy the game."
Michael Jordan

Idea 60: Learn How To Present to an Otter Personality

The Otter is a playful, fun loving people person who loves to make things happen. This personality type makes up about 15% of the population.   He is expressive, likes to talk, is very spontaneous and is somewhat disorganized. He is said to be the best promoter on the planet, initiates conversations easily, sometimes exaggerates and is a story teller.

Otters are typically sales people. They are very animated, laugh a lot and tell jokes, like fast cars, are fast paced and are people oriented. They are typically always moving and on the go and are into relationships.   The Otter is into the big picture as opposed to details.

145

The keys to presenting to Otters are as follows. They are spontaneous and make quick decisions. Make your presentation fun and get to the point. To those that are of a slower orientation, Otters may come off as obnoxious. Understand that they are conceptual thinkers so they may be steps ahead of you in visualizing applications for your offering that you haven't even presented to them.

And if you are an Otter yourself, create the relationship, present quickly and enjoy the spontaneity.

....

Today's Action Step: When presenting to an Otter, make sure you're ready to get to the point, anticipate some distractions along the way, and prepare to invest in a long term relationship.

....

To learn more, please visit www.ScottSchilling.com

Quote of the Day

*"It's not the size of the dog in the fight,
it's the size of the fight in the dog."*
Mark Twain

Idea 61: Learn How To Present to a Golden Retriever Personality

The Golden Retriever is a lover and not a fighter. This personality type makes up about 35% of the population. He is a friendly who loves relationships. He hates confrontations, is into nature and at the end of the day, just wants to take his clothes off and relax. He has pictures of his family close at hand in the office or in his wallet.

Golden Retrievers are family oriented, typically have plants, flowers and things of beauty surrounding them and love the great outdoors. They have a great desire to share, help and be part of a team. They tend to get walked over in their positions. They are definitely non-sales types and would fall into a support

147

role in customer service or like duties.

The keys to presenting to a Golden Retriever are as follows. Because of the pace and task orientation, you need to probably slow down, talk less and engage him in conversation. He believes he is a steward of our planet, and he is a care taker. He wants to feel warm and fuzzy.

You'll want to present slowly and ask Golden Retrievers a lot of questions to solicit their interaction. Ask their opinions frequently. And if you are a Golden Retriever yourself, you may never get around to the presentation or ask for the order because you will have such a love fest going on. You have to eventually get on point to get anything accomplished.

....

Today's Action Step: When presenting to a Golden Retriever, make sure you stay focused on the ultimate task at hand which is to present your offering and close a sale. Focus is paramount!

....

To learn more, please visit www.ScottSchilling.com

Quote of the Day

"Beavers do better work than the Corps of Engineers."
Mike Todd

Idea 62: Learn How To Present to a Beaver Personality

The Beaver is the worker bee, analytical and the master of detail. This personality type makes up about 35% of the population. He is the operations managers of the world. He has a strong desire to ensure things are done right. He wants a detailed analysis of the facts; once a decision is made he sticks with it. He is not touchy, feely or into hugs and feelings.

Beavers are typically the accountants, scientists and computer specialists of companies. They are the doers of organizations, slow paced and task oriented. They want everything on a schedule and tend to over analyze most situations.

The keys to presenting to a Beaver are as follows. They believe they need to review every fact and figure multiple times before making a decision. Because of the pace and task orientation, you need to give them everything you've got when it comes to details.

You'll want to present slowly because if you're too quick or slick, the Beaver will sense you are working to "slip something by them" even when you're not! If you are a Beaver yourself, prepare for paralysis by analysis to set in. You stand the potential to be in the battle of the detail for some time to come.

....

Today's Action Step: When presenting to a Beaver, make sure your presentation is highly organized, you have all the facts and are prepared by anticipating challenges along the way. This will take time so patience will be a virtue.

....

To learn more, please visit www.ScottSchilling.com

Quote of the Day

*"I made my own assessment of my life,
and I began to live it. That was freedom."*
Fernando Flores

Idea 63: Do Consistent Self-Assessments

No matter who you are or how long you have been in the sales world, there is always a possibility you can get a little stale, and there is always room for improvement. Just the fact our times and technology are changing so rapidly dictates that from time to time you need to step back a little bit and perform a self-assessment on what's going on.

Two of the best questions you can ask yourself, while rather simple and some would say common sense, tend to be overlooked without a little focus. So, here is that focus.

The questions are, "Is what you are currently doing getting you where you want and need to be?" And secondly if not, "What can be done to make the situation better?" These simple questions will start the ball rolling toward potential solutions.

Simply by asking the questions you open up your "reticular activating system," a part of the brain that automatically searches for answers once a question is posed. This approach creates possibility thinking or what is commonly referred to as "brain storming."

Let yourself go and write down whatever comes to mind. Don't judge what you have written immediately, keep writing. Once the thought flow has slowed or stopped, then go back and review what you have written critically.

....

Today's Action Step: Ask yourself the two questions above and write down whatever comes to mind. Don't judge or evaluate the thoughts until you have a list of about ten things. Then go back and critically review things more closely.

....

To learn more, please visit www.ScottSchilling.com

Quote of the Day

"To be idle is a short road to death and to be diligent is a way of life; foolish people are idle, wise people are diligent."

Buddha

Idea 64: Remember You're in the People Business

In virtually every training I present, the senior management of the organization first wants to drill home the point of the superiority of their company and offerings. While that is certainly a noble goal, it actually indicates a lack of understanding about why and how prospects choose to buy.

Product training has to do with why your nut and bolt is better than someone else's nut and bolt. Sales training has to do with learning the process and gaining the skills necessary to present your offering in a way you can sell more, with less effort, and make money doing it!

In reality, as a professional salesperson, you are in the people business. Once you understand this fact, it is far easier to execute the sales process. The reason is simple. Prospects do not buy what your offering does; rather they buy the benefits they will derive once they have made the purchase.

Their motivation to say yes comes from the fact that your offering will make them more money, reduce hassles, give them more time, provide them more choices and lessen their worries. That's what in it for them!

When you serve your prospects' needs first, understanding them as people, you will grow your business because your prospects will be "buying from you" versus "your selling".

....

Today's Action Step: Get to understand the five things prospects are looking for from the most recent customer surveys. They are more money, fewer hassles, more time, more choices and fewer worries. Understand the list completely and then review how your offering addresses these desires.

....

To learn more, please visit www.ScottSchilling.com

Quote of the Day

*"Anyone who has never made a mistake
has never tried anything new."*
Albert Einstein

Idea 65: When You're Wrong, Admit it Fast!

There are going to be times throughout your selling career when you are just flat wrong. You certainly did not set out to be wrong but for whatever reason, you were. If and when this situation arises, admit it and apologize immediately!

I've heard arguments such as, "I don't want to call it to their attention," or "It really wasn't that big of a deal." Quite frankly to keep it from being a big deal, you want to jump all over this and be the one to call it on yourself or your organization!

Inherently every one of us works to tell the truth, be upright and forthcoming in our presentations and business transactions. Whether you want to quote Murphy's Law or the more street

155

version, "stuff happens,"- stuff happens. When it does fess up, apologize and work to ensure it doesn't happen anymore.

A true sales professional values his relationships with his prospects and Clients to the point that he trusts in their relationship and does the right things at the right times for the right reasons.

....

Today's Action Step: Take a few moments to look back on your interactions and transactions with your prospect base. Critically evaluate if there is anything that hints at the possibility of a potential issue and address it accordingly.

....

To learn more, please visit www.ScottSchilling.com

Quote of the Day

"I like to think of sales as the ability to gracefully persuade, not manipulate, a person or persons into a win-win situation."
Bo Bennett

Idea 66: Know the Definition of Sales

Simply knowing the Webster's definition of sales will help you going forward. It sets a foundation for your mindset, and helps give you clarity of purpose. The Webster's definition states, "A sale is the exchange of a product, good or service for an amount of money or its equivalent."

Many times, a person like a chiropractor won't generally consider himself a sales person, but he is in fact doing exactly what the definition states.

He has a hard time when it comes to asking for money. The first suggestion in that case is to focus on the second part of the

157

definition, "or its equivalent." Exchange your product, good or service because "it makes your Heart feel good" (the equivalent).

An even more effective way to address "sales reluctance" is to adopt my "Heart-Centered Selling" definition of sales which is, "Education through Communication without Manipulation."

Simply put, adopt the perspective that you are an educator or a teacher who is sharing the benefits delivered by your offering to satisfy the prospect's needs, wants and desires. You are doing this through quality communication without resorting to any type of manipulation in the process.

Reframing how you perceive the sales process within your own mind now gives you a definition you can own and rally behind. Once you own it, you can execute it!

....

Today's Action Step: Adopt this definition of sales ["Selling is Education through Communication without Manipulation"] and put it into action consistently. Share your knowledge for the greater good!

....

To learn more, please visit www.ScottSchilling.com

Quote of the Day

"Networking is an essential part of building wealth."
Armstrong Williams

Idea 67: Network Where You Want To Be, Not Where You Are

Networking is a great way to increase your prospect base, grow your sales channels, and find a way to increase your market penetration. The challenge is most people network to and with the wrong "level" of networking partners.

Most sales people tend to network with those at their level and below, when in fact to grow their business, they need to meet and contact those who are above themselves.

This goes back to the study which concludes that we are all an assimilation of our five closest friends or business associates, and our performance is within 10% plus or minus their performance. In other words, if you want to do more and better business, learn to hang out and network with larger and better prospects.

Your time is a precious commodity, so make sure you are focused on "high leverage activities." These are the activities that give you the greatest returns for the time you have invested. If you truly have a desire to up-level the quantity and quality of your sales, make sure you up-level the prospects with whom you call and associate.

....

Today's Action Step: Critically review your networking practices and evaluate your level of success based upon the level of people with whom you are associating. In virtually every case, you'll want to stretch yourself.

....

To learn more, please visit www.ScottSchilling.com

Quote of the Day

"The best way to find yourself is to lose yourself in the service of others."
Mohandas Gandhi

Idea 68: Adopt Zig's Mindset

Back in the early '70's, long before ever officially starting a sales career, I was exposed to an amazing man by the name of Zig Ziglar. Zig is and has been the pre-eminent sales trainer for over 50 years.

While not remembering everything he shared way back when, there is one quote he made that will never be forgotten. In fact, it has been the foundation and driving force for my sales mindset and more importantly Heartset ever since.

The quote is, "You can have everything in life you want, if you will just help enough other people get what they want."

Zig's quote really typifies the Heartset of providing value to others by identifying their needs, wants and desires and delivering a quality solution to them. Jim Rohn supports Zig's stance when he states, "If you want to make more money, provide more value!"

When you adopt this servant leader attitude, work to provide a solution to your prospects' issues and put their needs, wants and desires above your own, you will undoubtedly create a more fulfilling and successful sales career.

....

Today's Action Step: Copy Zig's quote, "You can have everything in life you want, if you will just help enough other people get what they want" and attach it to your sales portfolio as a constant reminder of coming from a place of service to those you interact with daily.

....

To learn more, please visit www.ScottSchilling.com

Quote of the Day

*"Knowledge is like money: to be of value
it must circulate, and in circulating it can
increase in quantity and, hopefully, in value."*
Louis L'Amour

Idea 69: Feed Prospects the Food They Crave!

One of the best, fastest and most fulfilling approaches to create
and gain relationships with your prospects is to feed them the
food they crave. As a salesperson, your understanding of human
nature and what makes people tick will help you far more than
knowing your product inside out. That's not to say don't know
your product; what it is saying is know people and their
motivations.

Studies conducted by Les Giblin many years ago revealed that
everyone strives for three basic elements to feel good about
themselves.   Those elements are acceptance, approval and

appreciation.

To gain acceptance with your prospects, smile, listen intently, give them undivided attention and resist distractions. Your acceptance of your prospect breeds further acceptance of you. Once you've created acceptance, approval is the next step. While acceptance means tolerating something, approval means growing to actually like it.

People are always most interested in themselves. Talking with your prospects and really letting them share their interests is what speeds your way to approval. Showing a true desire for the prospect's benefit from a "helping others" orientation helps your efforts tremendously. Once your prospect feels approval, the next goal should be to invest further and show appreciation for your prospect whenever possible.

Give praise and recognition as often as possible. People will do far more for recognition than they will ever do for money. It's not what you give; rather it's how you give it!

....

Today's Action Step: Make a list of the people you can show some genuine appreciation to and then make sure you recognize them personally.

....

To learn more, please visit www.ScottSchilling.com

Quote of the Day

"Do the thing you fear most and the death of fear is certain."
Mark Twain

Idea 70: Understand Why Fear Holds Prospects Back

Fear is an interesting emotion to say the least. While we have all been naturally programmed with a certain amount of fear to be used for our own good, an abnormal amount can stand between you and becoming significantly successful.

On the positive side, fear is what keeps you on guard for hazards that pop up. It is gives you the ability to be alert and ready to take the appropriate actions necessary to stay safe. An irrational amount of fear however can and will absolutely stop people in their tracks.

Fear is nothing more than a conditioned response. It is very specific and a reaction to threat. Fear triggers one of three responses within you: fight, flight or freeze. You all know what fight is, when you tend to bow up a little bit. Flight conversely is when you have absolutely no desire to address the situation whatsoever. You're going to take off and move as far away as fast as you can.

Then you have your third possibility, and that's to freeze. Freeze is exactly what it sounds like. You get so afraid of the situation that you absolutely freeze and you don't do anything. Freezing can many times create the most hazards of all.

....

Today's Action Step: Take some time to understand the three ways fear is expressed: fight, flight or freeze. Connect how they potentially relate to your performance and prospect's reactions.

....

To learn more, please visit www.ScottSchilling.com

Quote of the Day

*"All the great things are simple,
and many can be expressed in a single word;
freedom, justice, duty, mercy, hope."*
Winston Churchill

Idea 71: Show Your Prospect Respect, Honor and Dignity

To truly create life long, quality relationships you must show respect, honor and dignity to your prospects. There are four simple factors you can apply. When you consistently put these into action, you will find a different level of respect, honor and dignity in return.

The first way to demonstrate and show respect, honor and dignity is through listening. Your prospect has a genuine desire to share detailed information to help you develop a solution for his issues. When you learn to ask quality questions, listen and he will deliver quality answers.

The second is to truly value the relationship and information your prospect provides. When you see this as valuable, and treat it as such, your prospect will grow to appreciate you and your capabilities more.

The third is by providing your undivided attention. We live in a society that values immediate gratification so much that the attention span of people continues to contract. Staying focused throughout your interaction will assure that your prospect "feels" you are with him.

The final element is to talk to, not through, your prospect. Make sure your presentation is at the level of the listener. If your prospect doesn't understand what you're presenting, he is not going to buy. It's just that simple.

....

Today's Action Step: Practice these four key elements for showing respect, honor and dignity around your workplace. Creating solid habits will carry out into the field.

....

To learn more, please visit www.ScottSchilling.com

Quote of the Day

*"If we lose love and self respect
for each other, this is how we finally die."*
Maya Angelou

Idea 72: Avoid Actions that Show Lack of Support, Honor and Dignity

Gaining a relationship with your prospects should always be a high priority. In business, just as in life, relationships can become fragile because of the interpretation your prospect applies to something you do during your interaction. That said, it makes sense to identify and become aware of the types of things that communicate a lack of respect, honor or dignity to the prospect.

The first non-verbal action could be something as simple as rolling your eyes as your prospect shares some information with you. This action can be interpreted as a sign of disbelief in the information shared and can damage trust in the relationship.

169

The second action is to stomp on or cut off your prospect's responses. Many times this coincides with not listening fully to what your prospect has to say. Either of these can and more than likely will be considered rude at the very least. More likely the prospect will feel you believe in your superiority to the extent you don't even want him to talk.

Another inappropriate response is to be condescending. No one likes to be talked down to, because again it is an indication you do not believe those you are talking to are at or above your level.

The final one is being impatient. Plan enough time around your meetings so you don't feel rushed or become impatient. This includes checking your mobile phone for incoming text messages. The prospect's feeling of importance will go a long way toward your having a positive outcome.

....

Today's Action Step: Ask those closest to you if there are times when you exhibit any of these characteristics. If so, learn from them and work toward eliminating them from your actions.

....

To learn more, please visit www.ScottSchilling.com

Quote of the Day

"Advertising is fundamentally persuasion and persuasion happens to be not a science, but an art."
William Bernbach

Idea 73: Be Persuasive in Your Presentations

To be truly persuasive in your presentations you have to express your information in such a way that is logical, emotional and motivational to spur the immediate action you desire.

Ultimately you have to affect your prospect's mind, his Heart and his will to encourage him to take action.

Your first consideration is the logical appeal. You must have a logical presentation of the facts. The left brain, the logical thinking side of the brain, will work to interpret your presentation sequentially, rationally, analytically, and objectively and will look at the various parts of what you have presented. You have to capture your prospect's mind.

171

Your second consideration is the emotional appeal. You must have an emotional appeal to your presentation of the benefits your offering provides. The right brain, the emotional feeling side of the brain, will work to interpret your presentation randomly, intuitively, holistically, subjectively and look at the whole effect of what you have presented. You have to reach your prospect's Heart.

The final consideration is building components into your presentation that will become motivational and inspirational to your prospect. He has total control over his free will. Your presentation needs to demonstrate why he should take action so strongly that he becomes motivated and inspired to take action immediately upon what you've presented.

....

Today's Action Step: Review your existing presentations and make sure you have included elements to satisfy all three of the considerations discussed. Is it logical, emotional and motivational?

....

To learn more, please visit www.ScottSchilling.com

Quote of the Day

"The soul never thinks without a picture."
Aristotle

Idea 74: Remember People Think in Pictures

Understanding how the mind works and using that knowledge in creating your presentations will go a long way toward your ultimate success. It is estimated that 65-70% of people are visual learners of some type. People generally think in pictures.

The mind is always thinking; studies estimate over 50,000 thoughts occur per day. This is one of the reasons positive self-talk is so important. In fact, the majority of the time the mind is thinking either in the past about events and situations that have already taken place, or in the future "visualizing" the desired result the person wants.

Rarely is the mind in the present unless it is especially focused and called to be concentrating on this specific moment at this moment.

Knowing this information, you have to grab your prospect's mind and "get them into the present." One of the best ways to accomplish this task is to present a picture that portrays the points you are working to get across in the presentation of your offering.

Create a picture that allows your prospect to actually "see" himself using your offering. Provide imagery to encourage the prospect in essence to "take ownership" of what you have to offer.

....

Today's Action Step: Get creative with your presentation and include more pictures than words to describe what you have to offer.

....

To learn more, please visit www.ScottSchilling.com

Quote of the Day

"A great many men's gratitude is nothing but a secret desire to hook in more valuable kindnesses hereafter."

Francois de La Rochefoucauld

Idea 75: Understand the Power of the Hook

Technically speaking, a "hook" is something that attracts attention or serves as an enticement for others to take notice. The desire is to relate to a prospect in a way that ensures he will give you his undivided attention for a period of time.

In a selling situation, it is a strong statement that causes a prospect to take note. An example of this type of hook would be, "Debt is painful" a statement designed to make the prospect's ears perk up.

Another type of hook is asking a specific question like, "What would you do with ...?" A direct question like this typically requires a response from your prospect and snaps him into the present as he considers how to answer.

And still one more hook could be a personal reference or celebrity testimonial. This reference creates a desire on the part of the prospect to use the product as well to "Be like Mike." This type of approach was used by Nike so successfully for so many years with Michael Jordan as one of their celebrity endorsers.

The final hook is the telling of a story or anecdote that becomes the precursor to your presentation. Your prospect "grabs onto" the story and now tracks along with you as you present your offering.

....

Today's Action Step: After reviewing the material above, take a few moments to develop a number of different potential "hooks" that can be incorporated into your presentation to improve its effectiveness.

....

To learn more, please visit www.ScottSchilling.com

Quote of the Day

"Basically, I have been compelled by curiosity."
Mary Leakey

Idea 76: Understand the Power of Salting

There is an age old saying, "You can lead a horse to water but you can't make him drink." Researching the origin and meaning behind the phrase, I discovered it is to portray the concept that like horses, prospects only have a mind to do what they want to do. Here's the most interesting thing about all of this - it is absolutely not true!

Quite the contrary actually. You can lead a horse (or prospect) to water, and always make him drink! How you're probably thinking to yourself? Well simply by "salting" their oats! You have to make them thirsty and when they are thirsty they will drink...with or without guidance from you.

Far too many times salespeople have the urge to purge every piece of information they know about their product, good or service. In actuality, to grow your business you need to become really good at making your prospect thirsty for more information. You want him to want more from you. You can easily accomplish this by creating intrigue!

Let your prospect fill in some of the blanks along the way. Certainly be there for him, supply the additional information he requests...after he asks you for it.

....

Today's Action Step: Think of the types of things your prospect would like to know. Be able to supply them when requested, but learn to encourage him to co-create a solution by making him thirsty in the process.

....

To learn more, please visit www.ScottSchilling.com

Quote of the Day

"Of all of our inventions for mass communication, pictures still speak the most universally understood language."
Walt Disney

Idea 77: Create Emotional Word Pictures

Starting your presentation with a story creates an instant image in the mind of your prospect. You can literally "paint him a picture" of what you are wanting him to consider. If I say to you, "Imagine if you will, the youth of today are lost like a puppy in a yard full of tall grass," you immediately create a vision in your mind of a puppy nestled down in a seemingly endless expanse of tall grass.

This statement immediately implants a vision and feeling. It allows you to see what I see, and feel what I feel, as I describe the situation. If I had said, "Today's youth are in trouble," you may have agreed with me. But it would not elicit the same type of emotion, response and ultimate buy-in for the solution about to be presented.

Emotional word pictures are analogies that your prospect can relate to from his frame of reference. "Others just like you have experienced the tremendous benefits this offering has delivered." You can see his smiling face. You can imagine how great he feels. You are relieved at the peace of mind he has achieved.

Bring instant clarity and power to your presentation through using emotional word pictures for your prospects that allows them to easily relate to the benefits they'll receive by saying, "Yes."

....

Today's Action Step: Create a number of different analogies you can call on going forward throughout your presentations.

....

To learn more, please visit www.ScottSchilling.com

Quote of the Day

"People take different roads seeking fulfillment and happiness. Just because they're not on your road doesn't mean they've gotten lost."

H. Jackson Brown, Jr.

Idea 78: Address the Top 5 Things People Are Looking for Today

We live and sell in an ever changing marketplace. Many salespeople feel like when they've just gotten a challenge figured out, it changes again. So true, and get used to it. There is nothing ever so constant as change!

A study recently released by marketing guru, Jay Shepard, detailed the Top 5 reasons prospects are taking action today. Knowing these and incorporating them into your presentations will certainly help you grow your business.

The number one reason prospects are taking action is because they have committed to purchasing the offering, and they have

181

been convinced it will help them make more money. Due to the issues in our world economy over the past few years, the ability to make money has moved to the top of everyone's mind.

Interestingly enough, the second motivator for action is to experience fewer hassles. Even though we live in this technological wonder age, we want less stress. Have you ever tried to program a new multi-media remote?

The third motivator is the recognition that we all share one commodity equally, and that commodity is time. No one is making any more of it, so it's literally time to use it more effectively. Everyone wants time back to do the things that are profitable, fun or rewarding.

The fourth is the opportunity to have more choice. Many suppliers have reduced the number of offerings in their product lines as a means of manufacturing efficiency. Prospects however are looking for more.

And the final reason in the Top 5 is to have fewer worries. Although this point is number five, if you can reduce the worry-load on your prospect, you will be elevated to a higher level.

....

Today's Action Step: Review how the features, advantages and benefits your offering delivers address the Top 5 motivators for prospects taking action, and incorporate them into your presentation.

....

Quote of the Day

"Life's most persistent and urgent question is, 'What are you doing for others?"
Martin Luther King, Jr.

Idea 79: Develop Open-Ended Questions

Every selling situation starts with two sides, you on the selling side and your prospect on the buying side. To ultimately have a successful transaction take place, there needs to be a meeting of the minds. Quite literally, each side must share enough information with the other side so that a positive decision is made to complete the purchase.

The interesting thing and unfortunately what many sales people either forget or fail to understand, is that everything they need to know to create a win-win transaction is in the mind of the prospect. And more importantly, they will share that information if you simply ask in a way in which they feel comfortable enough to give it to you.

To get this information, develop "open-ended" questions of your prospect. The simple definition of open-ended is any

183

question that cannot be answered with a yes or no, and will cause the prospect to elaborate on his position.

An answer to a question like, "Do you like this?" really provides very little information because the two easiest answers are, "Yes" and "No". And if you get a "No," you've just created more work for yourself.

Ask instead the question, "What did you like best about what you've just seen and heard throughout the presentation?" The natural inclination for the prospect will be to first give you an answer that is positive (because you designed the question to elicit a positive answer). Second the prospect will tell you the something he sees that is positive for them provided they take action. This is your goal!

....

Today's Action Step: Take some time to develop at least 10 open-ended questions you can learn to use on a consistent basis.

....

To learn more, please visit www.ScottSchilling.com

Quote of the Day

"Diamonds are nothing more than chunks of coal that stuck to their jobs."
Malcolm Forbes

Idea 80: "Know Your Outs" When You Get Stuck

Every great salesperson or even conversationalist gets stuck at one time or another. You're in the qualification process and have been asking such great questions, or simply sharing some ideal conversation when for whatever reason, you just go blank. You don't know what to say...you're stuck. That embarrassing moment of total silence can get pretty uncomfortable if it's your turn and nothing's there.

Well never fear, your answers are here! Over the years, I've learned a number of statements or concepts that have gotten me and so many of the people I have trained out of a jam when this situation has arisen. And oh by the way, if it hasn't happened yet, it will...prepare yourself like a pro.

One of the best "out" statements is extremely simple and therefore easy to remember: "Tell me more!" Your prospect is talking away giving you all sorts of detail on his latest project and the effect it will have, and you get stuck, simply reply "Tell me more!" Not only does it move the conversation along, it conveys interest in what you've been hearing.

A statement that gets your prospect into his creative brain is, "Paint me a picture" because that is exactly what he will start doing in his mind. Much like "paint me a picture" is something like, "What does that look like to you?" Again this will cause him to go visual and therefore emotional.

Two more quick ones that will both get you out of a jam, and get more information at the same time are: "Describe the perfect...car, house, solution, etc." and the extremely quick, "Really? Why?" Learning these and getting accustomed to using them when necessary can and will help your relationships grow.

....

Today's Action Step: Memorize the five "out" statements above; practice them with a member of your team and get proficient at calling upon them when necessary.

....

To learn more, please visit: www.ScottSchilling.com

Quote of the Day

"Take the first step, and your mind will mobilize all its forces to your aid. But the first essential is that you begin. Once the battle is started, all that is within and without you will come to your assistance."
Robert Collier

Idea 81: Know When to "T.O." the Sale

While every salesperson worth his salt believes he can close virtually every sale that comes his way, the fact is, there are times when he just can't. There are issues standing in the way when no matter how hard you try, or how good you are, you will not be able to conquer. Actually realizing, acknowledging and preparing for this is what shows you are a true sales professional!

The art of the "T.O." or turn-over is a developed skill that when used properly will actually increase your sales volume. There are five main reasons to T.O. the closing process to another.

187

The first reason is a conflict of personality or culture. These situations could be due to a myriad of reasons including gender, race or even background.

The second is due to a lack of product knowledge or to some technical reason. Basically the "sales process" has advanced outside your expertise, and you need to pull in someone else who can answer questions you can't.

The third reason is due to chemistry. You feel the presentation is not coming together as it should. You may or may not necessarily even know what's going on but whatever it is, it's not working.

The fourth is you definitely have a qualified prospect, meaning they have the need, want, desire and means to pay for it, yet you can't secure the enrollment. You have made numerous approaches that have not worked; it's time to call for reinforcements.

The final reason is to add a second voice. This approach is to confirm the enrollment and also congratulate your prospect on making a great decision.

....

Today's Action Step: Identify a team member who you feel comfortable with who compliments your level of expertise, and develop a system for "Turning-Over" sticky sales opportunities when appropriate.

Quote of the Day

*"A gift consists not in what is done or given,
but in the intention of the giver or doer."*
Lucius Annaeus Seneca

Idea 82: Adopt a High Intention, Low Attachment Attitude

This lesson alone could be the key to your exploding your sales business! It is gaining the understanding deep in your gut of the concept of "High Intention and Low Attachment".

I have been blessed to have learned this from a couple of great trainers, and more importantly fast friends, Jack Canfield and Robert MacPhee. It is a must lesson for those who want to grow your business.

The concept is actually quite simple. The first part is to hold the very highest of intentions for your actions. If your desire is to provide a quality solution for your prospect, visualize the result as if it has already happened. Feel how your prospect will feel as a result of this amazing transaction.

Do everything in your power and with all of your ability to ensure that the solution you will be providing accomplishes everything your prospect is looking for and more. Picture the entire transaction totally above and beyond reproach.

Now that you have established and "lived" that high intention, release it and allow the actions required to take place. You have created a high intention to the outcome; now create a low attachment to it working out exactly as you pictured. Know deep down inside if it is meant to be, it will be.

....

Today's Action Step: Continue the required actions, moving your project along without placing too much meaning as to how it will actually turn out. This approach will give you a greater peace about your efforts going forward.

....

To learn more, please visit www.ScottSchilling.com

Quote of the Day

"In order to succeed, your desire for success should be greater than your fear of failure."
Bill Cosby

Idea 83: Understand the Fear of Failure

The fear of failure is the fear of making mistakes or even losing approval. Many times it's tied to the fear of rejection in some way and ultimately becomes extremely self-limiting. You know, sometimes people say, "If I don't take action, I can't fail."

If you don't take action because whatever it is might not work out exactly right, you'll miss so many things that could be so fulfilling in your sales career and life.

It comes down to, "Who sets the rules?" Are you playing by your rules or are you judging yourself against somebody else's? Don't compare yourself. Don't compare whether you're better or worse. Failure is a distinction that you tend to hold within yourself.

Did you realize that when Thomas Edison invented the light bulb, there were 14,000 failed versions of that light bulb? Interestingly enough when Edison was asked about those 14,000 failed attempts, he put it in a pretty solid perspective. He said, "My good friends, there were not 14,000 failures on the way to inventing the light bulb. It was simply a 14,000-step process."

Is whatever you just experienced a failure? Or is it just part of the process? Buckminster Fuller addressed this concept extremely well. He said simply, "You can't learn less!"

Today's Action Step: Every time you do something, you have the opportunity to learn from the event. Get yourself into action and be persistent. Give it a chance. You're in action; keep going and "look for the good!"

To learn more, please visit www.ScottSchilling.com

Quote of the Day

*"I take rejection as someone blowing
a bugle in my ear to wake me up
and get going, rather than retreat."*
Sylvester Stallone

Idea 84: Understand the Fear of Rejection

The fear of rejection is the irrational fear that others will not accept you for who you are, what you believe or how you act. Fear of rejection can be a pervasive motivator for caution in behavior and interaction with others.

It's a state of mind that makes you incapable of doing or saying anything for fear of others' "rejection, lack of acceptance or disapproval." It's really a state of being overly dependent on the approval, recognition and affirmation of others to feel good about your actions.

Fear of rejection can rob your energy. It leads to self-immobilization and self-defeating, self-destructive behavior. It becomes the act of giving others more power than you give yourself.   Fear of rejection is an abdication of your own power and control over your own life. Left unchecked, other problems arise that often lead to self-dependence and codependent kinds of behaviors and situations.

Here's the exciting part. Rejection is only recognized within yourself! Nobody can reject you. The only one who can label anything as rejection is you. It's not what anyone says to you that causes this feeling of rejection. It is what you say to yourself after the other person has stopped talking! Eleanor Roosevelt said it many years ago, "No one can make you feel inferior without your consent."

....

Today's Action Step: Create a "brag book" or a "memory box" that stores all the positive comments and accolades you have received throughout your career. Then if anyone lobs something your way that you start to respond to as rejection, review the goodness that you have caused to happen, and take back your strength.

....

To learn more, please visit www.ScottSchilling.com

Quote of the Day

"Always bear in mind that your own resolution to succeed is more important than any other."
Abraham Lincoln

Idea 85: Understand the Fear of Success

You may be thinking, "Oh come on now, are you telling me I could possibly fear success?" Yeah, it is far more common than you would expect and happens all the time. The symptoms are telling. You have accomplished all that you desire, but you're still not happy; you still aren't content, and you still aren't satisfied once you reached the goal.

There's an underlying belief that you are undeserving of all the good things and recognition that have come your way as a result of your accomplishments and your successes. You fear accomplishment, being recognized and honored. That's right. You fear success.

195

Fear of success is the lack of belief in your own ability to sustain your progress and the accomplishments that you've achieved to this point in your life. It is an unnatural fear your accomplishments can potentially self-destruct at anytime. No matter how much you're able to achieve, for whatever reason you and others who have the fear of success believe it will never be enough, and you won't be able sustain it.

....

Today's Action Step: Create a journal detailing every success to date throughout your life. Take a look at the first third of your life, the second third of your life, and the most recent third of your life to date. It's amazing how many things you've accomplished! Give yourself the opportunity to celebrate your successes!

....

To learn more, please visit www.ScottSchilling.com

Quote of the Day

"Be a yardstick of quality. Some people aren't used to an environment where excellence is expected."
Steve Jobs

Idea 86: Create an Environment to Buy

For years I have encouraged salespeople not to sell anything to anyone, rather to create "an environment" for his prospect to buy from him.

While it sounds as if a transaction takes place in either situation, the orientation of where the decision making process is initiated is completely different.

If as a salesperson, you "sell" something to a prospect. You the salesperson are pushing the product upon the prospect. You may get the sale, but if there is ever any problem with the product, or the offering does not live up to the expectations that you created in presenting it, cognitive dissidence or buyer's remorse will set in. At that point, you have a problem!

Conversely, when you create an environment to buy, and the prospect feels comfortable in the purchase decision, they will pull the trigger and buy what you have to offer...in essence, pull it from you. Now if there are any unmet expectations, the customer will be less likely to create an issue and will be more likely to seek your advice and help on how to solve the issue.

They made the purchase decision; they are far less likely to be upset later on if there is an issue. They also get to take advantage of the "joy of ownership" because they were in control.

....

Today's Action Step: To create an environment to buy, ask quality questions to establish what the prospect is looking for. Present him with options he can consider to solve his situation.

....

To learn more, please visit www.ScottSchilling.com

"I think it's imperative to follow your Heart and choose a profession you're passionate about, and if you haven't found that "spark" yet, if you're not sure what you want to do with your lives - be persistent until you do."

Steve Kerr

Idea 87: Be Persistent

Persistence is one of the greatest attributes any professional salesperson can learn. The reason is simple; few times throughout your selling career will prospects say yes and purchase your offering with little or no effort on your part. When they do its great...it's called "a lay-down." While every salesperson alive would love to have "a lay-down" everyday, if that's your sales strategy, you're probably going to go hungry.

There was a recent study released by Notre Dame University regarding the persistence of salespeople in the sales environment. The study stated that 44% of the salespeople in the study quit calling on their prospect after the first unsuccessful call. Another 24% quit after the second unsuccessful call. Another 14% quit after the third unsuccessful call, and another 12% quit after the fourth unsuccessful call.

Totaling this up, 94% of the salespeople studied quit on or before the fourth unsuccessful sales call. What's the importance of the findings? Quite simply that another portion of the study showed that 60% of all buying decisions were made in the fifth call or thereafter!

It's not too hard to understand why the persistent salespeople (the remaining 6%) are so tremendously successful. In essence 6% of the salespeople had stuck around to service 60% of the opportunity.

....

Today's Action Step: Create a lead follow-up system that allows you to stay in touch with prospects to ensure that when they are ready to buy, you are available to them to sell.

....

To learn more, please visit www.ScottSchilling.com

Quote of the Day

"Everyone takes surveys. Whoever makes a
statement about human behavior
has engaged in a survey of some sort."
Andrew Greeley

Idea 88: Survey after the Sale

A great way to gain information after the sale is with the best two question survey I have ever learned throughout my 35 year selling career. It's pretty simple and something you can put immediately into your post sale or even post sales call routine.

"On the scale of 1 to 10, with 1 being the lowest and 10 being the highest, how did our organization support you in this transaction?" Or, "How is our product working for you?" Or, "How did you like working with us?"

Whatever that question might be, on the scale of 1 to 10, one being the lowest and 10 being the highest, how did we do?

201

If your prospect or now customer answers with anything other than a 10, the second question follows this statement, "Our desire is to have every interaction be a 10. In your opinion, how can we make it a 10?"

What you're doing when you perform this survey is very simply asking in essence, "What did we do well? And what do we need to improve on?" You are going straight to the people with whom you are doing business to give you the feedback you need to go from good to great!

....

Today's Action Step: Memorize and use this very simple survey so you can easily ask it of your prospects.

....

To learn more, please visit www.ScottSchilling.com

Quote of the Day

"Conformity is the jailer of freedom
and the enemy of growth."
John F. Kennedy

Idea 89: Understand the Four Ways To Grow Your Business

There are only four ways to consistently grow your business. Understanding them and putting plans into action based on this criteria will give you the momentum you need to increase your sales, make more money and grow your business.

The first way is to closely examine your customer base and clearly understand what they are buying from you currently, and how they could purchase or consume more of what they are already buying.

Once you identify your opportunities, plan and execute promotions or events to create more sell-through (sales growth).

203

The second is to examine your customer base and clearly understand which of their competitors could also be buying the same products yet would not hamper your original client's business. You need to know the market inside and out to identify potential opportunities for you going forward. Once you identify additional points of distribution in which you can present your offering, give those prospects the opportunity to come onboard (expanded distribution).

The third way is to closely examine your existing customer base and clearly understand what they are buying from you currently, and what else they could be buying from you if you could supply it. You need to know how to identify potential opportunities within your current customer base. Once you identify what expansions you can present to your offering, give your Clients the opportunity to buy the line extension.

The fourth is to understand the entire marketplace and evaluate if there are potential points of distribution in which you are not currently doing business. They may become an opportunity if your organization develops additional offerings outside the current offering (expanded offering).

....

Today's Action Step: How well do you know your Clients, their competitors and their needs? Do a critical review of your area of responsibility and determine where your opportunity for growth presents itself.

....

Quote of the Day

"All men dream, but not equally. Those who dream by night in the dusty recesses of their minds, wake in the day to find that it was vanity: but the dreamers of the day are dangerous men, for they may act on their dreams with open eyes, to make them possible."

T. E. Lawrence

Idea 90: Dare to D.R.E.A.M

As a constant-learner, I've been blessed to review, learn, and teach a tremendous number of courses taught by the best of the best regarding how to get into and stay in action.

While providing value, none gave me an easy to understand and act on formula for taking action and achieving success. So with that, I created the Dare to D.R.E.A.M. concept.

D.R.E.A.M. is an acronym for the five steps to take and stay in

205

action.

The "D" stands for Decide on Your Future. This is your life and you are the pilot. You can have anything you want in life; you just have to find someone who already has what you want and then do what they do.

The "R" stands for Restructure Your Activities. Make the changes necessary to be consistent with where you want to go, not where you are today. Your focus needs to be on the future because you get what you focus on.

The "E" stands for Execute the Plan. Most people fail because they don't create a plan in the first place. As the old saying goes, failing to plan is planning to fail. Create a plan and execute it.

The "A" stands for Analyze the Results. You have to "inspect what you expect" so there has to be the ability to measure your progress. Look honestly at your efforts and results. Everyone has lulls in activity and desire; don't be too hard on yourself.

The "M" stands for Modify the Plan and Re-Execute. It is unlikely that everything you put into action initially is absolutely perfect. And even if it is, our changing times will dictate your response accordingly.

....

Today's Action Step: Go through the five steps of the Dare to D.R.E.A.M. process and map out your plan for success.

....

Quote of the Day

*"When you're curious, you find
lots of interesting things to do."*
Walt Disney

Idea 91: Be Interested not Interesting

Not long ago I heard a concept that was so simple and yet so poignant it needed to be included in these Ideas. It is, "Be Interested not Interesting." This concept is yet another way to state who is really most important in the selling situation. Hands down it is your prospect.

Too many times sales people let ego creep into the selling process. As my good friend Dr. Gilles Lamarche shared with me a while back, EGO stands for "Edging God Out." Your Higher Source has a plan for everything you're involved in; let it play out. When ego takes over, the selling process is hamstrung.

This concept is not really about you as a salesperson, or even your offering for that matter. This opportunity has come about because your prospect has expressed an interest in your offering, and you happen to be the one fortunate enough to present it.

By acting on this concept of being interested and not interesting, you automatically subordinate your position in favor of your prospect's, and find out his needs, wants and desires. Once you do this, you now have the knowledge necessary to present to your prospect with quality.

....

Today's Action Step: Practice listening to one of your team members and simply keep the conversation moving without shifting the focus to you. Get accustomed to listening intently.

....

To learn more, please visit www.ScottSchilling.com

Quote of the Day

*"I made my own assessment of my life,
and I began to live it.
That was freedom."*

Fernando Flores

Idea 92: Look for the Opportunity in Every Event

In selling as in life, you are going to experience a tremendous number of events that cross your path. At first glance some are going to be good. Still others initially you may consider to be bad. In either case, how these events are perceived is totally controlled by one person - you!

Because the life of a sales person requires you to stay in a positive state of mind, that is if you want to continue to be successful and be welcomed by others, it makes sense to learn how to look at everything that crosses your path as an opportunity for growth. When you're green you're growing, and when you're ripe you're rotting!

The best way I have found to see everything as an opportunity is to ask these questions immediately upon the completion of the event: "What's the lesson in this?" "What is my gift?" "What did I do to create it?" And, "How can I make it better next time?"

At its most basic, asking these questions shows everything can provide a lesson (that's good); everything produces a gift (who doesn't like gifts?), and you get to take credit for creating it and understanding how you can improve it next go-round (nicely done!).

....

Today's Action Step: Take a few moments to think through some recent situations and determine your lesson, gift and contribution to the event's success. Put this Idea into action immediately!

....

To learn more, please visit www.ScottSchilling.com

Quote of the Day

"Action is the foundational key to all success."
Pablo Picasso

Idea 93: Understand the Cycle of Success

Four factors critical to the successful in selling any product, good or service. If you understand and act on any one of the factors, your business has the opportunity to grow.

The first factor is you have to have a "prospective market". There needs to be potential buyers for what you have to offer.

While on one side this seems fairly simplistic, on the other side it happens all the time - someone invents what he believes to be the next biggest whatever, and there is either no market for the product at the price or there is no market demand at all.

The second factor is you have to "pursue and engage" your prospective market. You have to be able to communicate to your prospective market the features, advantages and benefits your offering stands to deliver, and it needs to deliver what you claim it will.

The third factor is "performance and outcomes." After your offering is purchased, your new Clients use it as designed. If it lives up to expectation, there will be positive results, testimonials and ultimately referrals.

The fourth factor leads back to the first because it is your "passion and principle" regarding your offering. Your confidence and conviction in your offering becomes so strong you identify and explore new and better potential markets.

....

Today's Action Step: Think through each of the four steps and work to understand what can be done to provide a positive impact on any or all of the four factors.

....

To learn more, please visit www.ScottSchilling.com

Quote of the Day

"A market is never saturated with a good product, but it is very quickly saturated with a bad one."

Henry Ford

Idea 94: Know Your Prospective Market

The first factor in the cycle of success is to know the people who have a need for what you have to offer. You're very fortunate. It's very exciting to live on the earth where we live today because there are 7 billion people worldwide, 310 million in the United States, and 38.5 million in Canada alone.

You have plenty of "potential markets" to work. I'm not trying to suggest all 7 billion need what you have to offer. The point is that there sure are a lot of them that do!

The great news is we have a virtually unlimited market that exists for the products and services you have to offer. Clarifying who out of that 7 billion fits what you have to offer is the first key to success.

What are the target demographics that have a need, want or desire to partake in the benefits your offering has to deliver?

The greater clarity you can develop with regard to your target market, the more precise you will be in approaching that market with quality and pace. The more focused you are, the greater velocity you can achieve in penetrating the market.

....

Today's Action Step: Know the benefits your product has to offer inside and out, and then tie those benefits to the appropriate markets that have the desire and the ability to purchase your offering.

....

To learn more, please visit www.ScottSchilling.com

Quote of the Day

"All our dreams can come true,
if we have the courage to pursue them."
Walt Disney

Idea 95: You Have to Pursue and Engage

The second factor in the cycle of success is simply to pursue and engage your prospective market. You have to take some kind of action to identify the submarkets within that great potential market you already have.

You've got 7 billion people on the earth. As much as we'd all love to believe they all do, not all 7 billion are going to want what you have to offer. You have to learn to cultivate the market in a way that supports your plan.

First, you have to talk the talk. Talking the talk is fairly obvious. You have to know your products, your goods or your services completely. Furthermore, you need to be able to communicate the message about them effectively.

The second part of pursuing and engaging the market is far more important. That part is walking the walk. What's walking the walk? It's really important because as I learned from a great friend and associate Freddie Rick over the last number of years, "Your actions speak so loudly, I can't hear the words that you're saying."

It's not only about talking the talk; it's about walking the walk. Talk is cheap if you are simply dumping information without regard to how it is being received. Walking the walk is more of having your "words in action."

....

Today's Action Step: Make sure you are reaching the target markets you are intending to contact, and your actions are congruent with your communications.

....

To learn more, please visit www.ScottSchilling.com

Quote of the Day

"Confidence...thrives on honesty, on honor, on the sacredness of obligations, on faithful protection and on unselfish performance. Without them it cannot live."

Franklin D. Roosevelt

Idea 96: Know Your Performance and Outcomes

The third factor in the cycle of success is an understanding of your individual performance and its direct and indirect outcomes. The market has engaged and is using your offering, and with that your Clients have started to work with you at a much closer level because they are getting results.

Those positive results start to conjure up reasons for your customer to give you testimonials, and with a little bit of effort on your part, those testimonials will more than likely get you referrals. Referral marketing is huge because while the referral is not predestined to buy, he is at least predestined to listen. These referrals are already at least warm to what you have to offer. They have some knowledge of what you offer, who you are, and even why they should potentially do business with you.

Another thing to consider is the cost of a referral is typically zero. Most people like paying zero for a new piece of business. Referrals come with greater quality, cost less to acquire and are pre-determined to listen. This is a huge advantage going forward.

....

Today's Action Step: Understand your performance. Make sure you have some system established for capturing testimonials and referrals, and a way to use them both in your marketing approach.

....

To learn more, please visit www.ScottSchilling.com

Quote of the Day

"Great ambition is the passion of a great character. Those endowed with it may perform very good or very bad acts. All depends on the principles which direct them."
Napoleon Bonaparte

Idea 97: Develop Your Passion and Principles

The fourth factor in the cycle of success is the development of passion and principles. After you have successfully placed your offering into your prospect's hands, he will start putting it into action in his world with great success.

For you the net result of his success is what it does to build your passion and your principles for what you are doing even further. It gives you increased confidence and conviction in what you do and the offerings you present.

There's an old saying, "One man with a passion can do more than a hundred with an interest." When you embody those

219

passions, those principles, when you have that desire to truly make things happen, then you tend to go out and pursue your prospective markets with even greater fervor. When you do that, you "pursue and engage".

You gain additional "performance and outcomes". With that comes greater results, testimonials and referrals, which increase your passion, your principles, your confidence, and your conviction.

This process becomes a vicious "cycle of goodness". When you continue to do this, you cannot help but grow your business and your opportunities.

....

Today's Action Step: Build on your passions and principles. Then take a moment to step back from your day-to-day activities and "smell the roses." Celebrate the victories you have had and enjoy your efforts!

....

To learn more, please visit www.ScottSchilling.com

Quote of the Day

"A true measure of your worth includes all the benefits others have gained from your success."
Cullen Hightower

Idea 98: Create a Feature – Advantage – Benefit Presentation

There is an old cliché in selling that says, "You don't sell the steak; you sell the sizzle!" Similarly, for years in my training sessions I have said, "You don't sell what it is; you sell what it does!" To completely understand this concept and achieve a better quality presentation, you need to understand the strategy behind the "Feature - Advantage – Benefit" presentation.

To help you understand this conceptually, apply this question to the Feature - Advantage - Benefit model. "What - does it do - for the customer?"

A "Feature" is merely a thing. All sorts of manufacturers put all sorts of things in their offerings. But again, they are only things.

It's the "What" in this question, "What - does it do - for the customer?"

The "Advantage" is something good about the thing. It's what makes one manufacturer's thing better than another manufacturer's thing. It's the "does it do" in this question: "What - does it do - for the customer?"

The "Benefit" is what the customer actually needs, wants and desires. It is the feeling, sensation, affect and result that the customer derives from purchasing the thing. It's the "for the customer" in this question: "What - does it do - for the customer?"

A "FAB" statement for **"Without Clients"** might look something like this:

"Without Clients" (the thing – "What")

provides solid, quick and easily executable lessons (the advantage – "does it do")

so you can make more money, faster with less effort!" (the benefit – "for the customer!")

....

Today's Action Step: Create your own "Feature - Advantage – Benefit" statements designed around your offerings.

....

To learn more, please visit www.ScottSchilling.com

Quote of the Day

*"For, usually and fitly, the presence
of an introduction is held to imply
that there is something of consequence
and importance to be introduced."*
Arthur Machen

Idea 99: Introduce Yourself with Purpose

You only get one chance to make a first impression. You better make sure that you make a great one! So many times when walking up and meeting someone for the first time, a person will introduce himself by his job title or position. He'll say; "I'm Dr. Tom; I'm a Chiropractor", or "Hi, I'm Bill, and I'm an insurance agent".

While being either a Chiropractor or insurance agent is certainly a noble profession (industries in which I train and support significantly), what if the other person he has introduced himself to doesn't believe in or like that profession. You guessed it, within seconds he has potentially hampered this relationship getting off the ground.

What if instead he introduced himself like this: "Hi I'm Tom. I help people like you and families like yours live a longer, healthier, happier life for the rest of their lives." Or, "Hi I'm Bill, and I help people like you and families like yours enjoy the peace of mind that comes with knowing their futures are taken care of." What do you think is the first response in either case?

Yep—it's the exact same. "How do you do that?" Your introduction to someone new should be designed so that he wants to learn more about you, what you do, and how you do it. You have to create a little curiosity and intrigue. Your purpose is to have your new prospect and his curiosity asking you to tell him more.

....

Today's Action Step: Review how you introduce yourself presently and explore modifying your approach to be more effective using the format detailed above.

....

To learn more, please visit www.ScottSchilling.com

Quote of the Day

"He listens well who takes notes."
Dante Alighieri

Idea 100: Write Down Information Your Prospect Gives You

As you are finding out information from your prospect that could become very critical to your presentation later on, ask for permission to take notes as you are talking. As you start your qualification process (asking questions to learn about your prospect, his business and his needs, wants and desires) simply ask the prospect if he minds your taking notes.

In most cases, this action will be looked on favorably because you care enough about what the prospect is sharing with you to write it down. It actually shows a measure of sophistication in your process.

It demonstrates respect that what the prospect has to share is of value. One net effect is it helps the relationship grow because of the image of care and concern you create over what you are being told.

The other side of writing things down is you now have accurate information to use as you prepare and make your presentation. Writing notes gives you the ability to restate information back to the prospect at the appropriate time with integrity.

If throughout the presentation there is ever a point of disagreement about the "facts," you can refer back to your notes. You will be able to show the details are correct; you're not missing any details; the information came from them, and you are working to solve the stated issue.

....

Today's Action Step: Make sure you always take a note pad or portfolio with you so you can take notes and document the important details of your conversations.

....

To learn more, please visit www.ScottSchilling.com

Quote of the Day

"An objection is not a rejection; it is simply a request for more information."
Bo Bennett

Idea 101: Understand Objections Happen

In every selling situation, there is an exchange of information from the seller to the prospect. With every exchange of information, there is the possibility of one side or the other understanding the information differently from the other. By its very nature, this fact will create objections. They will happen.

Although many salespeople fear objections to their presentation, the objections themselves are only as much of an issue as you, the salesperson, chooses to make them. That's right, you are in control of how you choose to look at and address them.

In most cases, an objection is not really a true objection to your offering or presentation; rather it is a response and request for you to provide additional information to help the prospect clarify what he is thinking. When you look at objections in this light, they become nothing more than supplying further information.

Objections are only really a problem if you are not prepared for them. And as a professional salesperson, you would not think about making a sales call without being properly prepared, now would you?

....

Today's Action Step: Take time in advance of presenting your offering to practice responding to the most common objections that will be raised. Typically these include money/price, concerns from a significant other, time, effort to be made and concerns about quality.

....

To learn more, please visit www.ScottSchilling.com

Quote of the Day

"A place for everything and everything in its place."
Benjamin Franklin

Idea 102: Learn the "Franklin Balance Sheet" Close

One of the oldest and most successful closing techniques that has been around for years is the "Franklin Balance Sheet" method. It's important to learn this process because it is a very fair and forthright approach to detailing all the positives and all the negatives involved with purchasing what you have to offer.

Simply take a piece of paper and draw a line down the middle of the page vertically. Then close to the top of the paper draw a horizontal line across the paper.

On the upper left hand side (above the line and to the left of the center line) write the word "Disadvantages." On the upper right hand side (above the line and to the right of the center line)

229

write the word "Advantages".

Now that your paper is prepared, you simply guide your prospect through the process of listing what he sees to be the disadvantages of taking the action you are requesting of him. Let your prospect supply his input to ensure everything that is of concern gets written down.

Next guide your prospect through the process of listing what he sees to be the advantages of taking the action you are requesting of him. Let your prospect supply his input to ensure everything that is of benefit to him for taking this action gets written down. Knowing your offering, you may be able to help him see some additional advantages that he may not have mentioned himself. Typically, the visual confirmation of more positives than negatives helps your prospects see why they should take action.

With this task completed, use the positive nature of the advantages to address the concerns of the disadvantages. In most cases, the pluses will far outweigh the minuses.

....

Today's Action Step: Get with a member of your team and practice detailing the disadvantages and advantages your offering delivers. Use the Franklin Balance Sheet process to make sure you anticipate as many things as possible to gain the experience you need to feel comfortable.

....

To learn more, please visit www.ScottSchilling.com

Quote of the Day

*"In sales, a referral is the
key to the door of resistance."*
Bo Bennett

Idea 103: Always Ask for Referrals

One of the strongest prospects you will ever have is someone who has been referred to you by another trusted friend or associate. Immediately a number of wonderful things are put into action and start working in your favor.

The first thing that happens is you immediately gain credibility with the prospect because you leverage the goodwill, trust and reputation of your referral partner.

He obviously has a relationship strong enough to share the referral in the first place. Knowing that people associate with those they know, like and trust, you just assumed a portion of "the know, like and trust" that has been established between

231

those parties.

Secondly, although referrals do not necessarily come pre-determined to purchase, they do typically come pre-determined to listen. You have actually made it through one of the toughest stages of selling, past the gate keeper, because your referral partner has opened the gate for you!

You now have an opportunity to potentially present your offering, because the prospect that was referred must have some interest in what you have or he would have not acted on the referral in the first place.

Remember before you ever attempt to present, it is still your responsibility to ask the prospect questions to find out what he potentially needs, wants and desires from your offering, your organization and you.

....

Today's Action Step: Work to obtain referrals. Then treat this interaction with the care and respect it is due, because a trusted resource of yours has introduced you to a trusted resource of his!

....

To learn more, please visit www.ScottSchilling.com

Quote of the Day

"Let's choose today to quench our thirst for the "good life" we think others lead by acknowledging the good that already exists in our lives. We can then offer the universe the gift of our grateful Hearts."

Sarah Ban Breathnach

Idea 104: Be Grateful

One of the greatest lessons a salesperson can learn is to be grateful for every introduction, every interaction and quite frankly, every little thing that has happened both personally and professionally throughout his life.

Gratitude is tremendously powerful when you stop to think about it. Expressing even the tiniest amount becomes a game changer.

Tony Robbins has been quoted as saying, "When you are grateful, fear disappears and abundance appears." It is so true;

233

the power of gratitude is amazing. There's another reason to be publicly grateful based on a pretty simple premise. Why should your Higher Source grant anything more into your life if you are not happy and content with what you already have?

We all have been put on this earth to prosper and help each other prosper. Collectively we can all make our world a better place by starting from the foundation that we have each been individually blessed.

We are blessed to have what we already have, experience what we have already experienced, and learn what we have already learned. Now is the time for you to become even more aware of all the things in your life for which you are grateful and to express your gratitude more freely and openly.

....

Today's Action Step: Write down five things everyday for which you are grateful. Start each one of the gratitude statements with, "I am so happy and grateful now that...." Make this into a consistent daily habit and watch how your personal and professional life will improve!

....

To learn more, please visit www.ScottSchilling.com

Claim Your Destiny

Hopefully at this point, you have come to understand that you can BE anything you want to be. More importantly, you were put on this earth to have a fabulous life and live the life of your dreams. I also truly believe that we all have a second invitation while here, and that is to help as many people as we can along the way. My gut tells me you have that same desire, or you wouldn't have made it this far in the book.

Not long ago, I had the pleasure to share the stage with a great teacher and speaker by the name of Keith Cunningham. His presentation was awesome in so many ways. Toward the end of his talk, there was one thing Keith said that absolutely stopped me in my tracks. He was talking about everyone's individual potential and finished the point by saying, "Hell on earth is meeting the man I could have been!"

It absolutely pierced me to an all new and deeper level. Think about how profound those words are, "Hell on earth is meeting the man *I could have been!*" It begged the question, "Are you living up to your full potential and being all you can be?" I realized I wasn't; are you? You have been given so much talent, so much good, so much capability and the exciting part is all you have to do is put it into action. The tools to your success have been granted in advance and now you can truly claim your destiny if you have the desire to do so.

Wow, how interesting is it that as I write this, Jana Stanfield's amazing song, "What would I do today if I were brave?" is playing on my iPod? God, the Universe, Higher Source, the Law of Attraction really do have an amazing way of sending messages consistently when you're open to hearing them - literally!

As much as I would like to be able to say I have always been ahead of the curve in claiming my destiny, I have not. And I'll bet you haven't either. You know what? It's okay, in fact it's perfect! Why is it perfect you ask? That answer is simple. Your success is predestined in a grand plan and is going to happen exactly when and how it is supposed to happen. Like the old saying, "When the student is ready the teacher appears!"

It truly happens when you have a big enough *what* (you want to do), and a strong enough *why* (you want to do it), and with those in alignment, the *how* (it's going to happen) shows up. Kind of seems like it's showing up for you right about now doesn't it? You gotta' love when a plan comes together!

Abraham Lincoln said, "Always bear in mind that your own resolution to succeed is more important than any other one thing." In other words, your purpose, your passion for being here is far more important than anything else. The reason is fairly obvious, because you have your best interest at Heart. Henry Ford said it another way. He said, "Think you can, think you can't, you're right either way!" You can accomplish anything in life you desire. You just have to be clear on what you want to accomplish and take continual action toward that desire.

Rules of Life

How do you get there? Let's take a look!

Rules of Life

In a recent Advisory Council MasterMind meeting with 18 CEOs, presidents and senior executives from around the country lead by International MasterMind expert John Dealey, I was honored to be the host for the day. What that really means is I was in the "hot-seat" for the day presenting the business case study that I wanted to gain input on from this illustrious panel. As part of the preparation, John suggested that I detail my ten rules of life. These are the tenets of life which guide me and by which I live. It was truly eye opening to take some time, reflect and get really deep inside myself to determine what really makes me tick.

As it turned out, my rules of life are fairly simple, common sense and straight forward. In all reality, they are derived from a variety of influences throughout life including modeling my parents, what has been learned from a significant number of wonderful mentors, and one of the most memorable quotes I learned as a young pup. It hit me way back mid-70's, while reading Zig Ziglar's "See You at the Top!" It was Zig's quote, "You can get everything you want out of life when you help enough other people get what they want." It's amazing how sometimes you don't even realize how big an influence something has been over so many years.

That being said, here are my *10 Rules of Life*.

Be faithful to God's plan.

It is my belief that Higher Source has an ultimate plan for our success. For me that is God and Jesus Christ, for you it may be

Buddha, Allah, Hindi, the Universe, whatever you chose to call your Higher Source. To me it is naïve to think that we have been put here on earth and left to our own devices. With that, it is up to me to stay in the passenger seat and stop trying to grab the steering wheel to take control. When I act in alignment with spirit, it's absolutely amazing what happens! There is so much evidence daily that everything is happening at the perfect time for the perfect reasons. And as much as I'd like to take credit for them, many of these things are way beyond my scope to design and humanly achieve.

In every situation, look for the lesson.

There is a lesson available to you in everything that happens in life. When you anticipate this and are actively looking for that lesson, you stay in a place of constant and never ending personal improvement. It doesn't take long to again count your blessings for the sometime strange things that happen to you. Be a passionate learner and enjoy the childlike curiosity that comes along with it!

In every situation, look for the gift.

Just as with the lessons above, there is a gift in everything that happens as well. The exciting part about this mindset is that people naturally love gifts! While the lessons are educational and have the ability to help you set new courses of action going forward, the gifts are truly that, gifts. They are unexpected or unanticipated bits of pleasure, joy, prosperity, you name it!

In every situation, acknowledge your part in the creation of it and explore the potential for modification to the better going forward.

Give yourself credit for your part for initiating the wonderful results that have been created! You deserve to revel in your success. You've worked hard to accomplish what you accomplished, enjoy it! And as you savor your victory, take a reasonable look at the result, and explore if it can be made even better in the future through some modification. This is not to discount your success but to leverage it and build upon it. Make sense?

Maintain "Positive Discontent."

This to me is a far more optimistic and positive way to term what a friend of mine had in his Rules of Life which stated "Never be satisfied." You have to celebrate your victories and feel good about what you have accomplished. Maintaining positive discontent is more a feeling of "excited anticipation" that while you are pretty darn good at what you do and who you are, there is still more in you waiting to come out. Encourage that growth consistently!

Be a vessel for the message.

To be a vessel you really have to be congruent in all aspects of your life. Being the vessel entails everything from talking the talk, to walking the walk, to as Mohandas Gandhi said, "Be the change you want to see in the world." You are a walking talking delivery system of the message you want to share with the world. And that's not part of the day, week or month; it's all the time 24/7/365/forever!

Inspire and empower others daily.

Inspiring others is to help them be "in-spirit", just as you are in that spirit. Empowering them is helping them and sharing the tools they need to accomplish their dreams and visions. When you give inspiration and share empowerment, those you touch certainly benefit. You'll find very quickly the true reward comes back to you tenfold or more. Be that source of good in the world and you will be amazed at how good you feel!

Integrity is job #1.

By definition, integrity comes from the integer "1". It is wholeness. A complete and whole presentation of who you are every minute of every day. That means whether you are at home with your family, on the road working with a bunch of cronies, no matter where or what you are doing or who knows you are doing it. Unfortunately we see this in the world far too often from those many people viewed as role models who fall from grace due to infidelity, ponzi schemes or just plain not keeping agreements. All you really ever have to do is ask yourself, "Will the potential fallout from being out of integrity be worth it?" Ask Tiger Woods and Bernie Madoff - probably not!

Be present and enjoy the day.

This is one that I have really struggled with in the past because as a high achiever, I've worked much of my adult life to "make things" happen as opposed to "allowing them" to happen. When talking to many others, I feel like many people are thinking about what happened in the past, or where they are working so hard to get to in the future, that they don't stay present in the current time and really enjoy the day. One of the keys for me that has made this easier and better is to refer back to rule number one and understand that all this is in the master plan anyway, so enjoy every bit of it to the fullest every day!

Strive daily to insure the 14 inch journey.

This is a daily check up from the neck up. Where are you coming from throughout the day? Is it from your head being extremely tactical and less feeling? Or is from your Heart with an understanding that doing things for the right reasons at the right times is a huge part of fulfillment? It is a definite goal of mine to stay in my Heart 100% of the time, and I'm committed to continue to make progress toward that end until I'm no longer here on earth.

Do you have a written statement of your 10 Rules of Life? If not, you may find it an extremely valuable exercise to discover more of what makes you tick. Bet you find out a few things about yourself you didn't realize before, and more importantly develop one heck of a track to run on from this time forward.

Many times it has been said, "Life is not a destination, it's a journey". How true! The most interesting thing about that is we are all in control of how we view it. It is within our individual mindsets. We are the most unique beings on earth. We have been granted so many gifts that allow us to experience our surroundings in so many wondrous and mysterious ways.

Enjoying life is the reward that everything else we do is wrapped around. Growing, learning and expanding consistently has made my life more enjoyable. The changes you will accomplish by putting what you have read in this book into action will amaze you. They will be neat, exciting and all that. What you will really achieve is the capacity to live more fully in all aspects of your life. Your mind, your body and your spirit will hit new highs that will become the benchmarks for your future!

My wish for you is to achieve whatever it is you want to achieve in your life. You are absolutely amazing as you are today. The exciting thought is that where you are is only the beginning of what you are going to BE. And more importantly, the levels you will achieve, the inspiration you have become and the number of people you have positively impacted along the way will create a ripple that can truly be felt around the world!

No matter if your desire is to become highly successful, or simply understand this information better to help others you care about, congratulations on your journey! Thank you for the honor of sharing this with you. You too can be an inspiration to so many. Please let me know how I can be of service to you toward your progress going forward. Have fun!

Let's Sum it UP

You made it - congratulations! Hopefully you have recognized how the ideas and action steps in "Without Clients" can be put into action immediately and help you achieve the sales growth you want to accomplish. I appreciate your investment in yourself by taking the time to read the information provided and listen to or watch the ideas as they are delivered via email.

If you wish to discuss any of the ideas or just want to let me know your thoughts, get in touch via my blog at **www.ScottSchilling.com**.

So many others have expressed what great value they've received through the training within this system. They have passed along that their greatest successes have come by taking action on what they've learned. My suggestion is put these ideas into action, and do it now! It makes no sense to wait or put this off until tomorrow, your business needs action!

With these ideas fresh in your mind, you can plan how you are going to implement them daily to improve your level of success. You now have greater tools to grow your skill set, your mind set and your business.

One last thing, please review the resources page. There are a variety of links and information that may be of interest to you to augment your approach to the market. These tools will help you solidify the relationships you have achieved, help you gain new opportunities and increase your bottom line in multiple ways.

If you would like to share "Without Clients" with anyone you know who you feel would benefit, we've provided some images and tools to make sharing this information easy for you. There is even an affiliate program that rewards you should you decide to take advantage of what is available.

I'd love to hear your thoughts. If you have any comments about this program which you like to share your comments, please go to **www.ScottSchilling.com**. I'd love to hear from you!

Thank you again for your interest, enthusiasm and commitment to yourself and those you touch!

To Your Increasing Success!

Scott Schilling

Tools and Downloads

Share with others - it's free, easy and profitable!

Recognizing that people always refer things they like to others, it only makes sense to create an incentive for you to share "Without Clients" with those you know who can benefit. We've added a "tools and downloads" section to reward you for promoting "Without Clients" with a significant commission. If you would like to create some additional income, the process is really very easy.

Simply follow the three step plan below and start collecting 30% commission on every affiliate sale from "Without Clients."

Step 1—Login to http://www.learnfromscott.com by entering it in your web browser
Step 2—Go to the "Affiliate Signup Section"
Step 3 – Use the promotional material provided to advertise "Without Clients."

Sharing the message

There are many ways you can advertise and share the message of "Without Clients" to others who have a similar desire to improve their ability to "Grow Your Business." Some of the easiest to implement are listed below:

- Advertise your affiliate links on Facebook, Twitter and/or any of the social media platforms.
- Place a banner ad or graphic on your website, blog or other public posts.

- Add your affiliate links to your communications or email signature.
- Send a pre-written direct campaign to your mailing lists or subscribers.
- Direct others to **www.ScottSchillingRecommends.com** through your affiliate link.

If you have any questions or any other ideas that you'd like to discuss regarding sharing the message of "Without Clients," please feel to get in touch through the website **www.ScottSchilling.com**.

Check out the resources from "Without Clients"

Please find below a list of helpful resources.

Contact Systems to "Stay In Touch"

eMarketing System— http://www.VideoPromotionsNow.com

- This system has unparalleled capabilities, all in one place and at a great value.
- This platform allows you to communicate more effectively with your prospects, Clients and vendor partners.
- Increase your brand awareness and your profits. This platform helps create brand awareness in online business marketing by combining traditional marketing tools with modern technology, such as video-enabled email campaigns allowing you to take full control of your online business marketing efforts.
- Included are tools to successfully measure and refine your marketing efforts, and you get the most complete Internet Marketing System available.
- Build and maintain better relationships by personalizing all of your customer and client contacts with video.
- Make business or organizational presentations with slides and guest speakers using live or recorded broadcasts.
- Manage and publish your pictures and videos.
- Create your own web pages without using a hosting service.

- Collaborate with associates with shared contact lists, calendars and documents.
- Capture leads with web forms or with text messaging. Follow up with campaigns and auto-responders all with robust reporting.

Automated "Card System"—
http://www.ReferralsBuildBusiness.com

- This system allows you to schedule consistent "touches" with your prospects, Clients and vendor partners. There are thousands of pre-designed greeting cards (Thank You, Birthday, Holiday, etc.) across all areas of business and occasions. You also have design capability to create your own personalized messaging. There is even an option to be able to have the message appear in your own handwriting for the sake of personalization.
- From the comfort of your own computer you can create a single card or an automated campaign sending thousands of cards in a matter of minutes. Once you create the card(s), it is printed, stuffed in an envelope, addressed, has a physical stamp affixed, is delivered to the post office and mailed for typically less than the cost of a "store bought" card.

Business Growth Systems

Instant Income Small Business Plan—
http://www.createinstantincome.net

- This comprehensive new business plan reveals the little-known, income generation strategies developed for the world's top celebrity entrepreneurs.

- These 101 "Instant Income" strategies are designed to immediately put cash in your bank account.
- If you need to get more Clients... increase sales revenues... boost cash-flow... or jump-start your new business development... you can instantly download this business plan designed to bring in cash in just hours, days or weeks.
- Over seven information-packed sections, you'll learn, in thorough detail, the strategies for finding more Clients...in more places...with help from more people than you ever imagined.
- You'll discover the proven methods for selling these Clients more products and services over a longer period of time.
- You'll learn how to plan your cash-flow generating activity - and how to track your results and response rates.
- You'll cut through the overwhelming and confusing excess of Internet marketing "strategies" to discover the simple, time-tested 5-page website system that continually attracts traffic and converts visitors to sales.

Website Design and Hosting—
http://www.TurnKeyWebSolutions.net

- This PLUJO platform allows you to communicate more effectively with your prospects, Clients and vendor partners through website design and hosting.
- PLUJO was created by a team of highly experienced website developers and marketers.
  Their positive and negative experiences have culminated in the product that is now PLUJO; high quality servers and networking, stable and efficient email system, and secure and safe data storage.

- With PLUJO your need for a hosting provider is completely removed. The PLUJO servers will host and deliver your website using their premium and reliable platform. Premium servers on one of the world's most stable networks are used to ensure that your website is delivered to your visitors quickly and consistently.
- Email services are also included with your monthly PLUJO subscription and are based on the same high quality networks provided by Rackspace. POP, Imap and webmail access to your email is permitted, and all email is protected against SPAM and viruses using industry leading technology.

eLearning System—
http://www.SuccessThroughEducation.com

- Learnopia is a complete online learning solution.
- Learnopia is a learning management system (LMS) in which teachers create, host, and sell (or give away for free) their online courses.
- Many eLearning courses are free, and the rest are affordable, as low as $9.99.
- Affiliates can earn a "lifetime" of extra income by letting others know about them.
- Learnopia saves money and lowers risk.
- There are no hosting fees, merchant account fees or software license fees.
- You receive increased reach to worldwide audiences.
- Affiliate transactions are made for you.
- An automatic database collection of contact information is provided.

- Available is 24/7/365 access to learning material for purchase /delivery around the world.
- A fee only occurs for service after products are sold.

Additional Recommendations—
http://www.ScottSchillingRecommends.com

- There are so many wonderful products, opportunities and organizations these days that truly have fantastic offerings that I have learned about and grown to trust. Just like my commitment to my mentors to share the information they have taught me over the years, I feel a similar commitment to these products, opportunities and organizations.
- To inform others about my "Trusted Resources," I organized them into one of three categories: "Organizations" I train or work with (so I have some input in the quality of their presentation); "Products" that I have personally used on an ongoing basis; and/or "People" I have grown to trust over years of working with, studying and being together. These are my "Trusted Resources."
- There is a shared philosophy of helping others, making the world a better place, and using our collective talents for the greater good. As I meet more quality suppliers of information, products, goods and services, this reference will continue to grow to share the benefits with more people consistently.

http://www.PrePlannedFacebookPosts.com

Use it to:

- Schedule future posts from inside Facebook
- Schedule posts that repeat
- Post to multiple pages & groups at once
- Target posts by language and geo-location
- Access over 4000 pre-written status updates in our status database (created just for fan pages)

Sign up now and get:

- Your brand and icon under every post
- A link to your website under every post
- Unlimited use on all your pages and groups
- An app built exclusively for you!!!

Affiliate Disclaimer:

From time to time, I will promote, endorse, or suggest products and/or services for sale. My recommendation is ALWAYS based on my belief that the product and its author will provide excellent and valuable information or service based on a review of that product, my relationship with that person, and or previous positive experience with the person or company whose product I am recommending.

In some cases, I will be compensated if you decide to purchase that product based on my recommendation. In some cases, I will receive the product for free for review purposes. Always do your own due-diligence before making any purchases. Never purchase anything that you cannot afford. Most people don't do anything with the products they buy, so most of the time, their typical results are zero.

About the Author

Scott Schilling...**Business Growth Expert**

Scott Schilling is the founder of Schilling Sales and Marketing, Inc. - an organization committed to providing **Inspired Answers to Today's Challenges** through sales training, consulting, coaching and implementation strategies. Bottom line, Scott helps individuals like you and organizations like yours grow market penetration, improve profitability and grow the quality of your people.

Scott brings 30+ years of life experience in sales, marketing, training, and speaking to corporations, business owners, and entrepreneurs. His expertise is delivered through speaking, coaching, business consulting, live workshops and sales trainings, webinars, written articles and books.

This is his life's purpose: **To inspire and empower others to serve humanity through living their life's purpose in spirit, love and joy!**

Through his affiliations with Fortune 500 companies, innovative start-up companies and high paced individuals, Scott brings a wealth of knowledge, sales, marketing, implementation strategies, education and expertise to the podium and to print. Scott's books to date include, *104 Tips to Grow Your Business, Talking With Giants!, Thank God I..., Expect-a-Miracle, GPS for Success, Extreme*

Excellence, Conversations on Success and *Wake Up...Live the Life You Love.*

As an Internationally accomplished and entertaining presenter, Scott has spoken to thousands of attendees across a range of industries. He has made over 1,250 live presentations recently in 6 years alone!

Scott's goal is to maximize the potential and God-given talents of the individuals and organizations he encounters. Delivering content in an easy to understand and digest style make his presentations extremely valuable because they can be implemented quickly by his students.

To contact Scott, he can be reached by calling at **(972) 659-8941**, via email at **Scott@ScottSchilling.com** or by visiting his websites at **www.ScottSchilling.com** or **www.ScottSchillingRecommends.com**.

Schilling Sales and Marketing, Inc.

4020 N. MacArthur Boulevard

Suite 122-183

Irving, TX 75038

(972) 659-8941

Other books written by Scott Schilling & Available at www.ScottSchilling.com

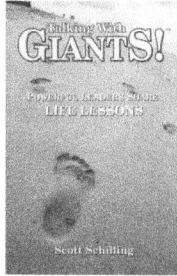

Talking With Giants! is a work that truly comes from the heart. It comes from gratitude and a true desire to help you feel the successes available to those who live from a place of service and generosity to others.

It came from a desire to support a particular charity (Habitat for Humanity) at a time when the author s personal financial resources were not available so another vehicle had to be created. It evolved into an understanding of how amazingly blessed we all are and that because of those blessings; we all have the opportunity to do more for others.

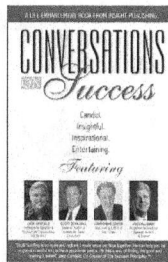

Most of us want to be successful. Some of us spend more time than others dreaming of success, planning for success, and working toward success. For some, success comes easy, almost naturally. For others, it is as elusive as a summer breeze. One thing is certain, countless men and women have beaten the odds and achieved remarkable success, and in doing so, have learned lessons that can benefit us all.

Scott co-authored this book along with Jack Canfield (Co-founder of the Chicken Soup for the Soul series), Joe Callaway and Joel Christiansen among others.

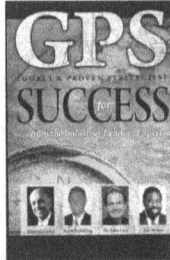

In this powerful edition of GPS for Success, some of America's most notable business professionals share their inspirational success strategies. So, pull up a chair and be prepared to learn. Your greatest successes may be just around the corner!

Scott co-authored this book along with Stephen Covey (7 Habits of Highly Effective People), John Gray (Women are from Venus and Men are from Mars) and Les Brown (World's Leading Motivational Speaker) among others.

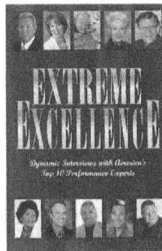

The bottom line really becomes making the decision that you want to change or improve where you are, you want to do something that makes you more fulfilled and happy in your life. It's that first decision that makes a huge difference. When you know where you want to be, more than likely there is somebody who's already there, somebody that you can model, somebody that you can learn from, someone that inspires you to want to be more and if you can take the same steps to get there, that whoever is already there took to get there. Then the reward is the journey and also worth the journey!

www.ingramcontent.com/pod-product-compliance
Lightning Source LLC
Chambersburg PA
CBHW061724270326
41928CB00011B/2101